Alphabet Zoo

"...Lions and Tigers and Quilts for You"

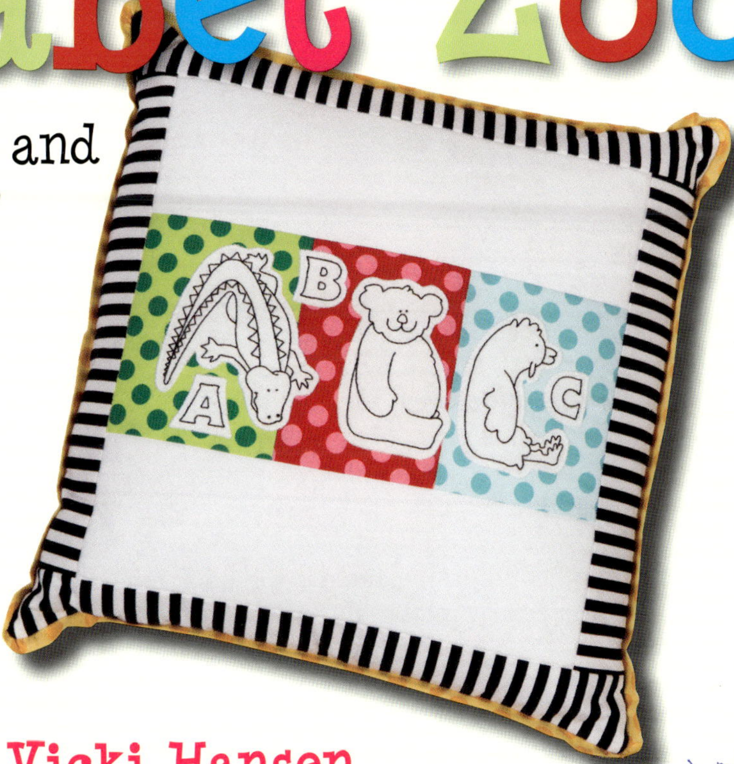

By Vicki Hansen
of Cranberry Pie Designs

For Suzanne: fellow Quilter! Have
fun with this book
Vicki Hansen

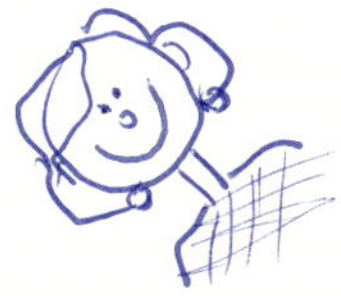

CRANBERRY Pie designs

Alphabet Zoo

"...Lions and tigers and quilts for you"

By Vicki Hansen

Editor: Donna di Natale
Designer: Renae Ronquist
Photography: Aaron T. Leimkuehler
Illustration: Lon Eric Craven
Technical Editor: Christina DeArmond
Photo Editor: Jo Ann Groves

Published by: Kansas City Star Books
1729 Grand Blvd.
Kansas City, Missouri, USA 64108

First edition, first printing
ISBN: 987-1-61169-126-9
Library of Congress Control Number: 2014935481
Printed in the United States of America
by Walsworth Publishing Co., Marceline, MO
To order copies, call StarInfo at (816) 234-4473.

KANSAS CITY STAR QUILTS
Continuing the Tradition
KansasCityStarQuilts.com

Star Stitch
THE KANSAS CITY STAR
StarStitchBlog.com

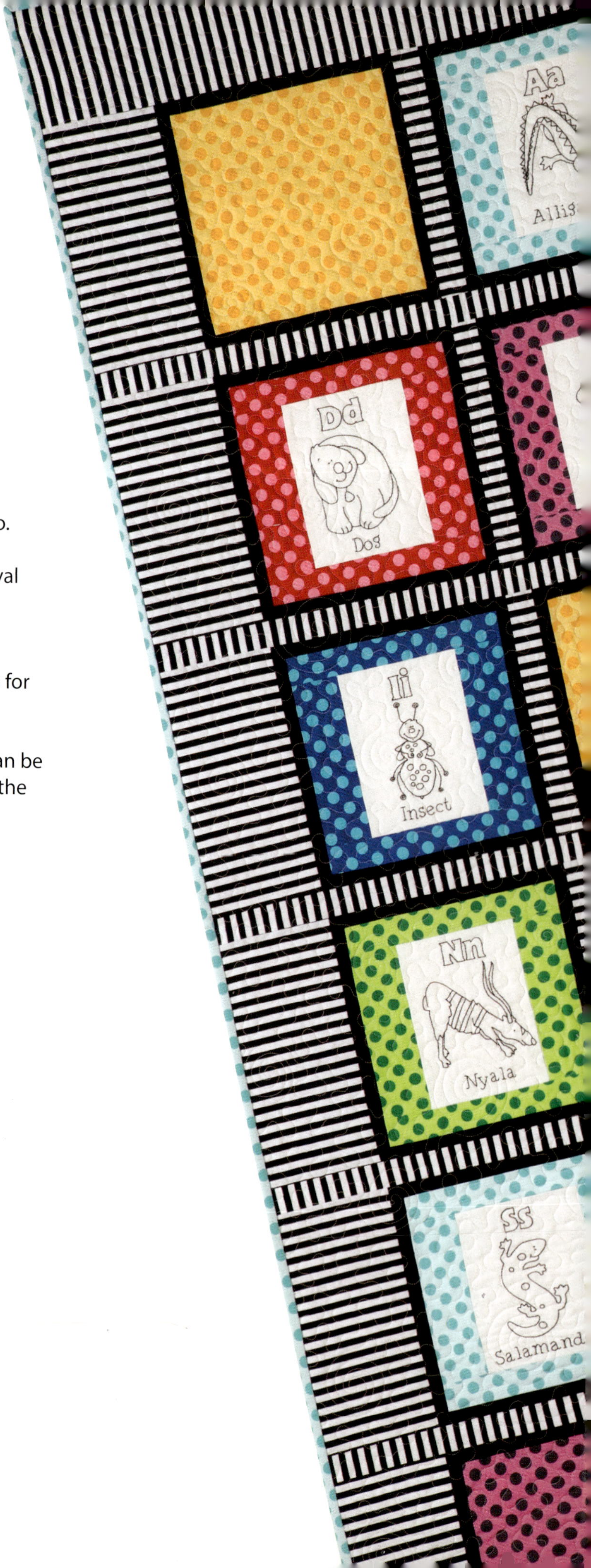

Table of Contents

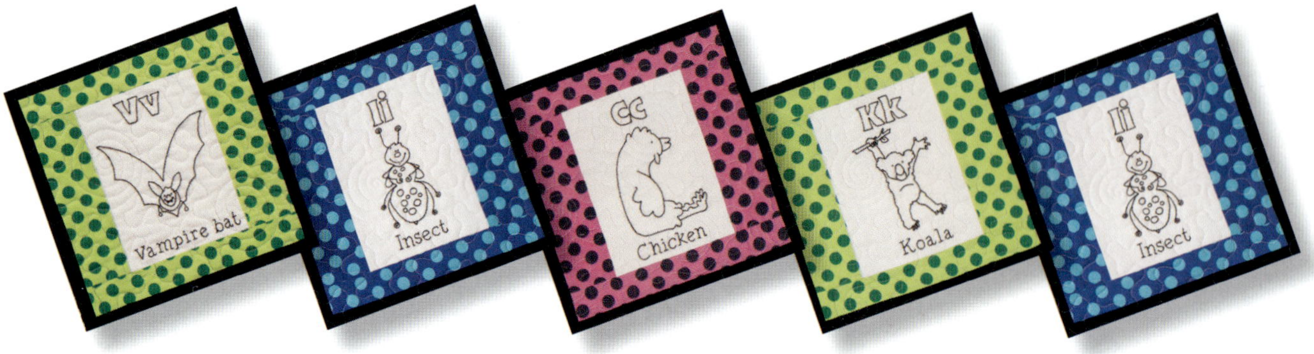

About the Author

Vicki Hansen was raised in the Pacific Northwest. After a four-year hitch in the U.S. Navy, she graduated from BYU and the University of Washington.

She currently works as a receptionist in a dental office, where she can be found working on quilt projects in the break room during her lunch hour.

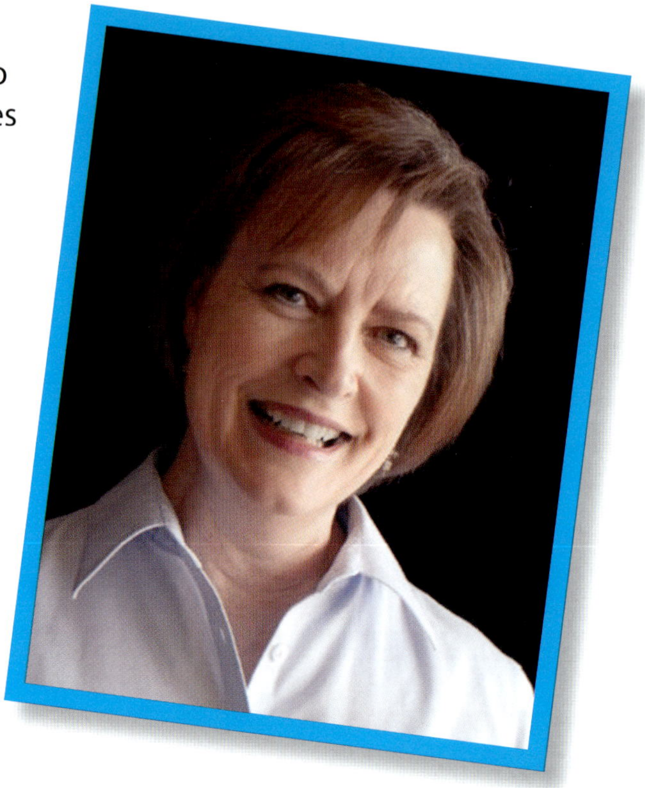

When not quilting, she loves to read, do puzzles and sing oldies rock and roll at the top of her lungs while riding in the car.

Vicki and her husband, Kevin, have three amazing children and three super-amazing grandchildren.

Vicki and Kevin live in Port Angeles, Washington, where they can see Victoria, British Columbia, from their living room window.

Robins, Corinne. "Ten Months of Rush Hour Figuration." *Arts Magazine 57(September 1982): 100-103.*

Sabbath, Lawrence. "Via New York Attacks Cherished Beliefs, Styles . . ." *Montreal Gazette,* 12 May 1984.

Schjeldahl, Peter. "Mind over Matter." *The Village Voice* 27(9 March 1982): 79.

——. "Art at the Gates of Hell." In *New Figuration in America,* Milwaukee: Milwaukee Art Museum, 1983.

——. "Bad Boy of Brilliance." *Vanity Fair* (May 1984): 67-72.

Schutz, Sabine. "Back to the USA." *Die Kunst* (December 1983): 827-834.

Smith, Roberta. "Everyman's Land." *The Village Voice* (26 October 1982): 98.

——. "Representation: An Abstract Issue." *The Village Voice* (11-17 March 1981): 75.

Spalding, Jeffrey. "Eric Fischl," In *Coasts, the Sea and Canadian Art,* Stratford, Ontario: the Gallery/Stratford, 1978.

——. *Aspects of Canadian Painting in the Seventies.* Calgary: Glenbow Museum, 1980.

Staniszewski, Mary Anne. "Group Drawing Show." *Art News* 80(March 1981): 232.

Storr, Robert. "Desperate Pleasures." *Art in America* 72(November 1984): 124-131.

Sturtevant, Alfred. "Outakes from the American Dream." *Island* (October 1983): 62

Tarzan, Dennis. "Self Portraits." *The Seattle Times,* 7 August 1983.

Tatransky, Valentin. "Eric Fischl." *Arts Magazine* 55(May 1981): 34.

——. "Fischl, Lawson, Robinson and Zwack: They Make Pictures." *Arts Magazine* 55(June 1981): 147-149.

——. "Death or Glory." *Cover* (Spring/-Summer 1981): 42-47.

Tousley, Nancy. "Canadian Painting: Aspects of the Seventies." *Vanguard* 9(Summer 1980): 30-37.

Tucker, Marcia. "An Iconography of Recent Figurative Painting: Sex, Death and Violence." *Artforum* (Summer 1982): 70-75.

——. "Paradise Lost/Paradise Regained: American Visions of the New Decade." In *La 41 Biennale Venezia.* Venice: United States Information Agency, American Pavilion, 1984.

Van Jurg Kupper, Hans. "Metaphysik des Alltaglichen." *Baseler Zeitung,* 11 June 1978.

Webb, Marshall. "Eric Fischl at Sable-Castelli Gallery." *artmagazine* 14(December 1982 January/February 1983): 39-40.

White, Stuart. *The Reality of Perception.* Newark, New Jersey: Robeson Center Gallery, Rutgers University, 1981.

Wylie, Liz. "Eric Fischl at Sable-Castelli Gallery." *artmagazine* 12(May/June 1981): 78.

Yau, John. "How We Live: The Paintings of Robert Birmelin, Eric Fischl, and Ed Paschke." *Artforum* 21(April 1983): 60-67.

Zimmer, William. "Theme Song (and Dance)." *SoHo Weekly News* 2-8 June 1980.

Honnef, Klaus. "Acht Monografien: Eric Fischl." *Kunstforum* 61(May 1983): 58-59.

Huser, France. "Sur la Baie de Narragansett." *Le Nouvel Observateur* (March 1984): 19

Jacobs, Joseph. *Faces Since the 50s.* Lewisburg, Pennsylvania: Center Gallery, Bucknell University, 1983.

Kuspit, Donald. "New York Painting Today." In *New York Painting Today,* 5-6. Pittsburgh: Two PPG Place, 1983.

____. "Eric Fischl's America Inside Out." *C* ((Winter 1984): 14-17.

____. "Eric Fischl." *Artforum* 20(Summer 1982): 85.

Lawson, Thomas. "Eric Fischl: Review." *Artforum* 19(May 1981): 72.

____. "Eric Fischl Review." *Real Life Magazine.* London, England: Nigel Greenwood Gallery, 1981.

Lehmann, Henry. "On Canvas from Sea to Sea." *Montreal Star,* 24 January 1975

Liebmann, Lisa. "Eric Fischl's Year of the Drowned Dog." *Artforum* 22(March 1984): 67-69.

Linker, Kate. "Eric Fischl: Involuted Narratives." *Flash Art* (January 1984): 56-68.

Lubell, Ellen. "Schnabel's Choice." *The Village Voice* (8 May 1984): 41.

MacKay, Allan. "The Maritimes." In *The Canadian Canvas,* Toronto: Time Canada Ltd., 1975.

Marshall, Richard. In *American Art Since 1970,* 5-17. New York: Whitney Museum of American Art, 1984.

Mays, John Bentley. "Eric Fischl Rages at the Giants of Art." *Toronto Globe and Mail,* 14 February 1981.

Owens, Craig. "Back to the Studio." *Art in America* 70(January 1982): 99-107

Paikowsky, Sandra. "Eric Fischl: Paintings." In *Eric Fischl: Paintings,* Montreal: Sir George Williams Art Galleries, Concordia University, 1983.

Perrin, Peter. "Friends of the Form." *artscanada* 35(February/March 1978): 44-47.

Pincus-Witten, Robert. "Entries: Palimsest and Pentimenti." *Arts Magazine 54(June 1980): 128-131.*

____. "Entries: Snatch and Snatching." *Arts Magazine* 56(September 1981): 88-91.

Racine, Rober. "Festival de performances du M.B.A.M.: Eric Fischl, Paul Theberge, Carol Wainio." *Parachute* 13(Winter 1978): 46.

Randolph, Jeanne. "Eric Fischl: Sable-Castelli Gallery." *Vanguard* 10(April 1982): 29-30.

Ratcliff, Carter. "Contemporary American Art." *Flash Art* (Summer 1982): 32-35.

____. "Expressionism Today: An Artist's Symposium." *Art in America* 70(December 1982): 60-62, 69.

____. "The Inscrutable Jasper Johns." *Vanity Fair* (February 1984): 61-65.

____. "Spain: The Structure of Ritual." *Vanity Fair* (March 1984): 58-66.

Rickey, Carrie. "Taste Test." *The Village Voice* (5 May 1980): 83.

Acknowledgements

Many, many thanks...

- To Kris Cornell, owner of Quilted Strait quilt shop in Port Gamble, Washington, who sold my first patterns and encouraged me to expand my quilting horizons.

- To Terry Tamaki, devoted friend, head cheerleader. With unfailing loyalty, Terry helped me tote my things all over Quilt Market where I first met the Kansas City Star Quilts group.

- To Jeanne Wolfley, an elementary school teacher friend, who first suggested that my personal "zoo" of animal drawings include animals that are shaped like the letters they represent.

- To Alynn Lowe, who asked me to draw a dolphin.

- To Robin Santino, for permission to use her elephant Zoo key photo.

- To my editor, Donna di Natale, for guiding me with patience and a sense of humor through the entire publishing process. And to the rest of the staff at Kansas City Star Quilts, for taking a chance on a first time author. I appreciate it!

- To the Johnson County (Kansas) Library, and especially the staff of the Lackman Branch, for allowing us to photograph the projects in their children's reading area.

- And finally, to my family – my children, Katherine, Karlan and Michael, and my husband, Kevin. I love you all so very much and appreciate the support and encouragement you've given me over the years that have made this whole adventure possible.

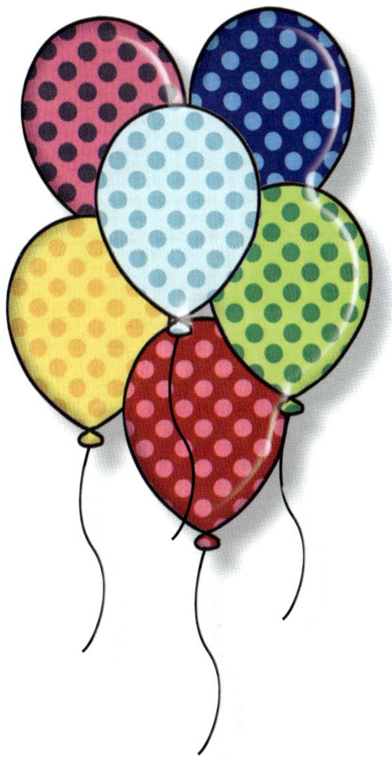

Introduction

You might say that the genesis for this book began in the mid-1960s when I was a young girl living in a small town about 45 minutes outside of Seattle. I loved visiting Seattle's Woodland Park Zoo with my family. Back then, admission was free; you brought along a bag of day old bread and some peanuts and coaxed the bears to wave at you.

One year for my birthday, my parents gave me a key to the zoo – or rather, a Zoo Key. This was a large plastic key shaped like an elephant with a long, vertical trunk. All around Woodland Park Zoo, metal speaker boxes, dubbed talking storybooks, were posted at various exhibits. You'd stick the trunk of the Zoo Key into the box, turn it, and a brief, rather scratchy sounding narrative about the animal you were viewing came to life. It was magic.

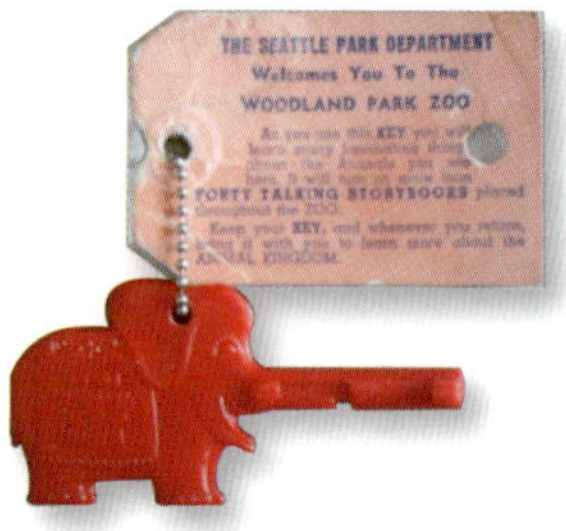

In that era of typewriters and reel-to-reel audiotapes, it seemed that the Woodland Park Zoo was really on the cutting edge, their Zoo Key boxes sheer genius. I recently learned that zoos all over the country once boasted similar boxes. A woman named Robin Santino has posted her massive collection of these zoo keys on Flickr. Robin's keys depict not only elephants of every color, but monkeys, lions and other creatures as well.

I've always enjoyed drawing, and fonts hold a particular fascination for me. While considering animals that could be shaped like the letters they represent, I thought back to some of the exotic and unusual animals I enjoyed visiting at Woodland Park. Nyalas, zorillas and jerboas soon joined my personal "zoo," along with the requisite bears and lions. Years later, when I took up quilting, the animals became the perfect foundation for a blackwork alphabet quilt. Alphabet Zoo is the result.

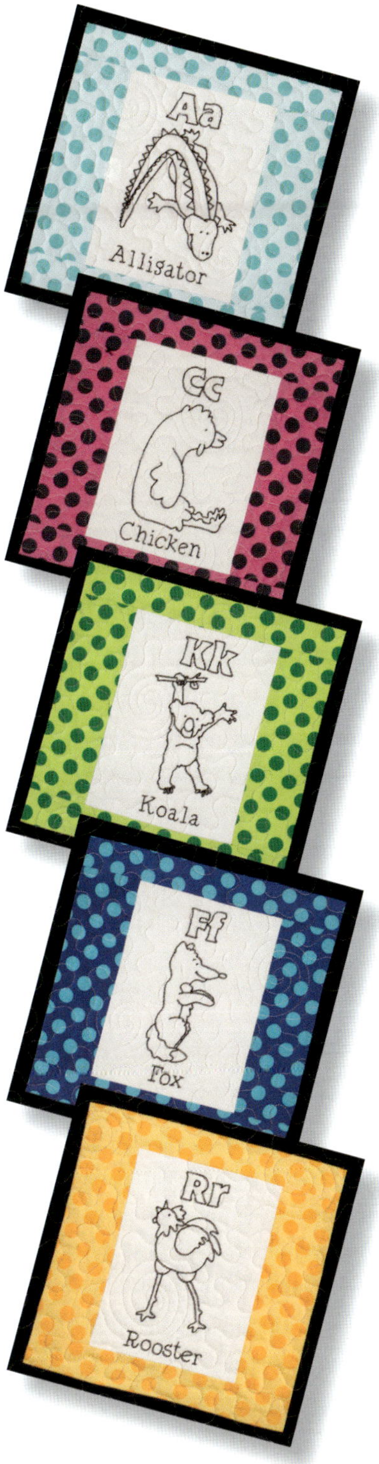

Your child or grandchild will have a great time learning their ABC's while cuddling up with the bright, happy Alphabet Zoo quilt showcased in this book. In addition, you'll find instructions for a personalized baby quilt, pillow, Happy Birthday banner, wall hangings and an embroidered pillowcase. Some of the projects are colored first, using simple crayons to achieve the vivid results; directions are included.

Full-size templates for the capital letters used for the Alphabet Zoo quilt can be found in the back of the book, as well as templates for an array of lower case letters, making possible an endless number of personalized embroidery and quilt projects. You might find yourself making plans to stitch up bunting for a crib set, a soft cover baby book, a bib, an alphabet banner, a book cover or a picture frame! I'd love to hear about your finished projects. Send me a note at vicki@cranberrypiedesigns.com.

Have fun!

Vicki

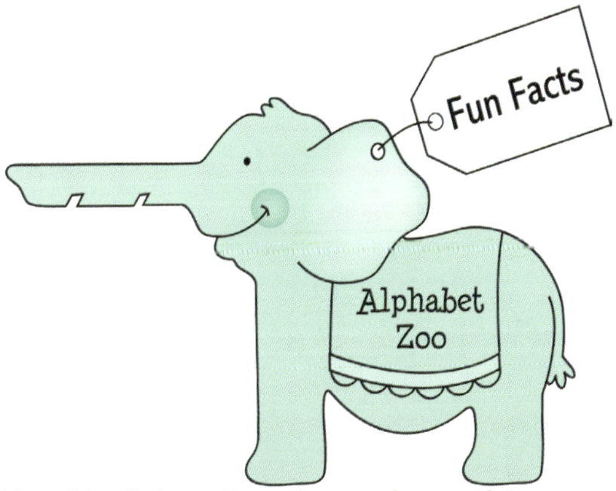

Look for the special "Alphabet Zoo Key" drawing throughout this book. It will be your guide for discovering fun facts about the animals featured on the Alphabet Zoo quilt. No scratchy metal speaker box required.

General Instructions

FABRICS

The majority of the fabrics used for the projects are from Michael Miller Fabrics: *TaDots* in Berry, Sunny, Cobalt, Peony, Grass and Sea, and *Clown Stripe* in White. Refer to the samples below for identifying the fabrics.

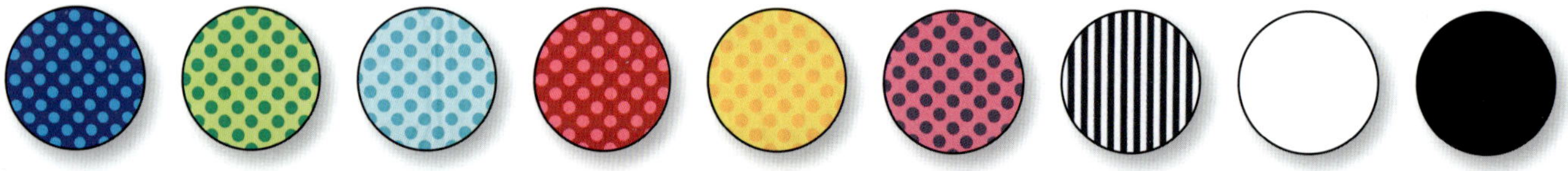

EMBROIDERY

All of the projects in *Alphabet Zoo*, except the pillowcase and Happy Birthday banner (which have separate templates), were created with the full-size alphabet letters on pages 57-73. You may wish to reduce or enlarge the letters with a photocopier to fit your individual needs.

The Roman letter font used for Olivia can be found on page 74.

PREPARING YOUR FABRIC

Use 100% cotton fabric. I recommend that you ALWAYS preshrink your fabric. I like to toss my fabric into the dryer after washing, but remove it while it is still slightly damp so it will iron easily. Press well before cutting.

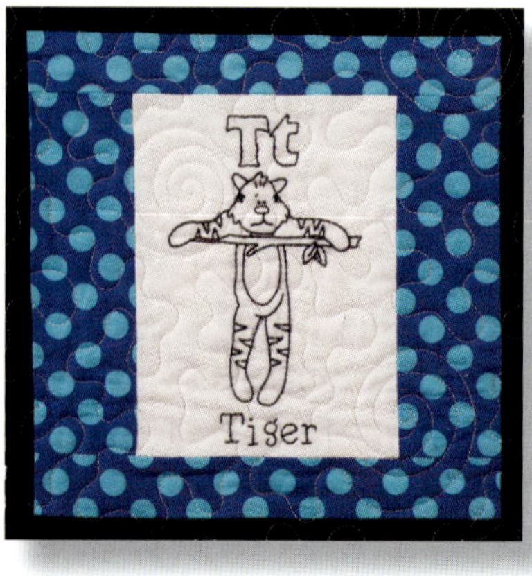

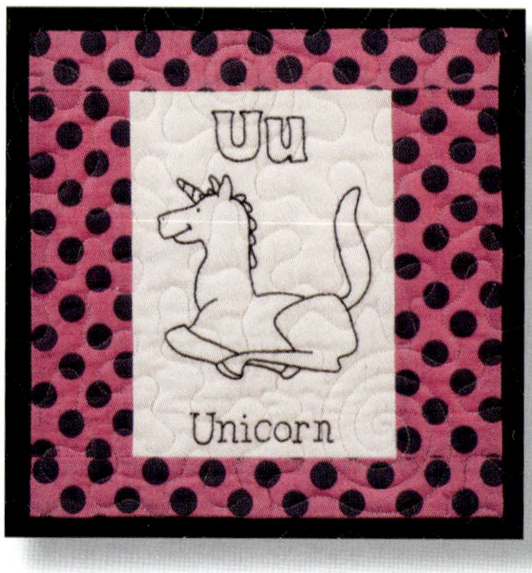

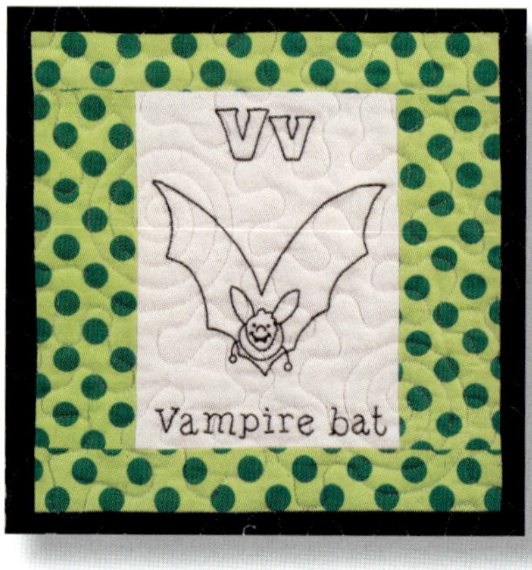

CUTTING FABRIC FOR EMBROIDERY BLOCKS

Cutting instructions are based on 42″ wide fabric and include a 1/4″ seam allowance unless otherwise noted.

Using a rotary cutter, cut each block to be embroidered to the pre-assembly size given in your pattern instructions. The larger dimension leaves room for ease when using an embroidery hoop, as well as allowing for some natural shrinkage that occurs as the block is filled with stitching. When the embroidery is complete, center the design according to the instructions and cut to the trimmed size, which includes the 1/4″ seam allowance.

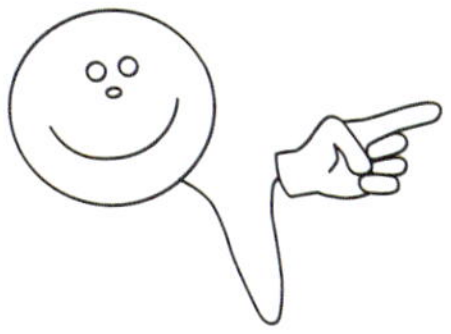

TIP: *I like to layer my embroidery blocks with muslin for stability. This is optional, but it makes a clean-looking finished block with no thread shadows. Cut the muslin as you would the block fabric. After your design is transferred to the block fabric, layer, smooth, and you are ready for the embroidery hoop.*

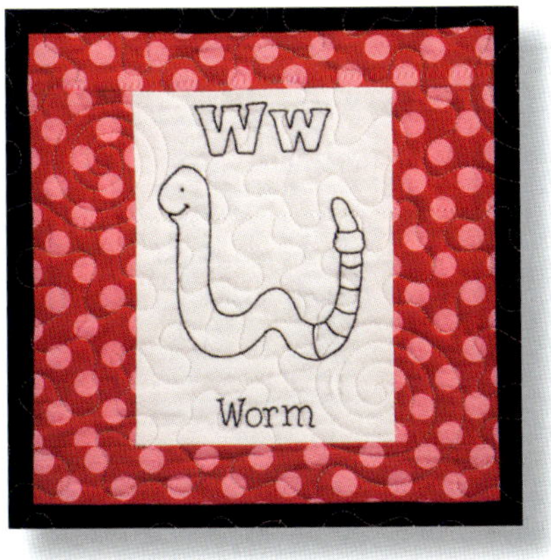

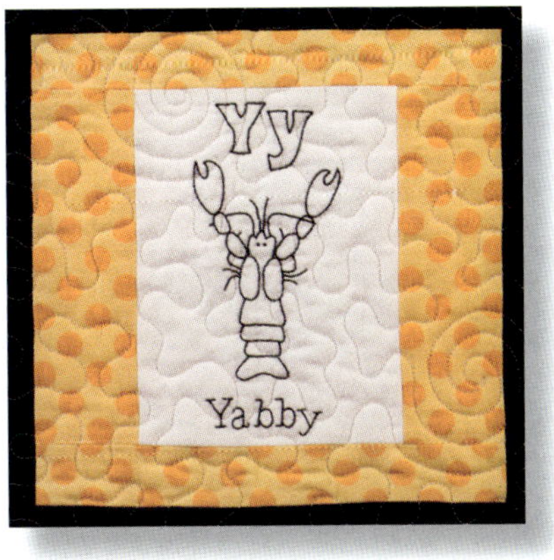

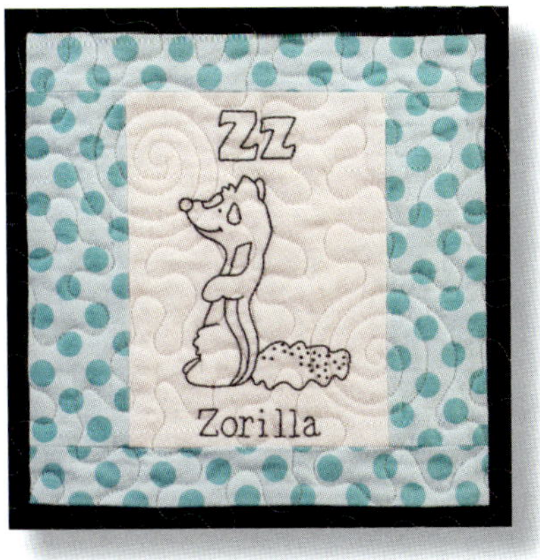

General Instructions continued

TRANSFERRING THE DESIGN ONTO YOUR FABRIC

• Trace the design onto your fabric with the aid of a light box or sunny window. Use a fine-tip pen for tracing.

• Pigma Micron pen, size .01. Brown ink is a good choice, but other colors are available. Iron your fabric after tracing to set the permanent ink.

• Heat sensitive pens, such as Frixion pens, are my personal favorites. They do not demand that you transfer your design or stitch with exactness. An iron or hairdryer will make the ink disappear. (You should be aware that the ink will reappear under conditions colder than 14° F. In that case, simply reapply heat.) "Ghost" lines may appear on dark fabric after the ink has been ironed away. These can be removed by dabbing with a damp cloth and a bit of dishwashing soap.

• Transfer film, such as Transfer-Eze or Fabri Solvy, creates a very accurate pattern. The pattern design can be scanned into your computer and printed directly onto the business side of the film. Peel away the paper backing and finger-press the film directly onto your fabric. Stitch as you normally would. When stitching is finished, the transfer film can be removed by soaking in cold water for 5-10 minutes.

STITCH AWAY!

• If you buy floss by the skein, separate and use two strands to stitch your design. Floss that comes on a spool or in a ball (I like to use size 12 floss of Perle Cotton) is needle-ready and does not need to be separated. Make certain the thread you choose is colorfast!

• Solid lines on your pattern are worked in a backstitch. Shorten your stitches as you go around curves to make smooth lines.

• Dots are stitched with a French knot. I usually wind my thread just once around my needle. Winding the thread twice will, of course, make a larger knot.

• As you finish each section, or come to the end of a length of thread, carefully knot the thread on the back of your work and tuck the loose ends into the rest of your stitching.

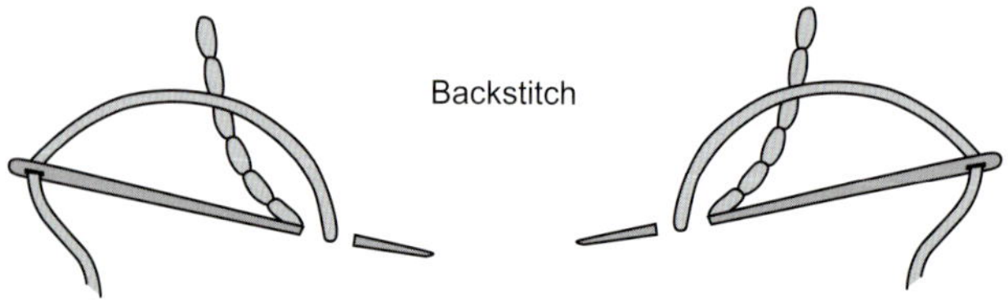

Backstitch

Left-handed Right-handed

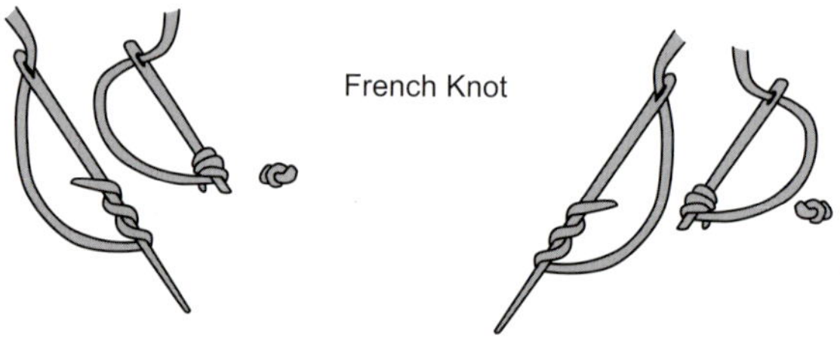

French Knot

Left-handed Right-handed

ASSEMBLE YOUR PROJECT ACCORDING TO PATTERN INSTRUCTIONS

• Press fabric carefully and square up, square up, square up! Taking time to press and square your work as you go along will greatly increase the ease and precision of assembly – and will make certain that your completed project looks neat and straight.

• Use 1/4" seams to assemble your project. Press seams toward the darker fabric unless instructed to do otherwise.

CARING FOR YOUR EMBROIDERY

• **Wash in cold water** on a gentle cycle. You might want to toss a sheet of color catcher in with your wash to prevent any possible bleeding. Dry on low or lay your work flat to air dry. Press carefully.

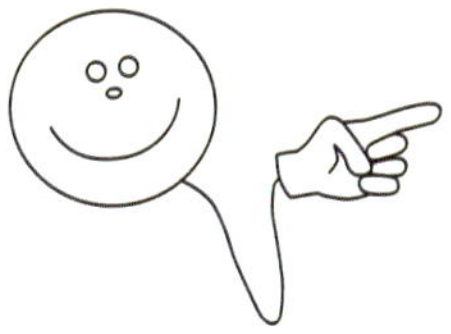

TIP: *Spritzing a bit of starch on the back of your embroidery blocks before pressing makes them look nice and crisp. A little bit of starch also prevents bias cuts from stretching as you sew. I recommend Mary Ellen's Best Press Clear Starch Alternative. It doesn't flake or leave a residue and doesn't attract bugs that might damage your quilt.*

ALLIGATOR

American alligators have between 74 and 80 teeth in their mouth at any given time, and each gator can go through 2,000 to 3,000 teeth during its lifetime.

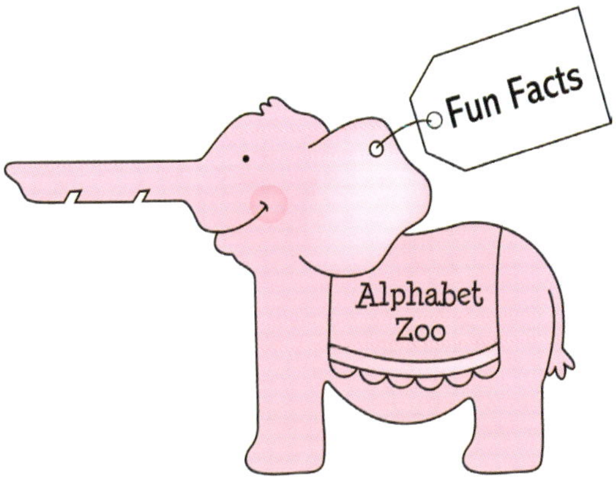

Instructions for Coloring Fabric with Crayons

1. Coloring fabric with paint, markers or crayons can be a fun part of the creative quilting process. I've discovered that crayons make a great foundation for my blackwork embroidery. The crayon is applied and then pressed with an iron so that it melts and becomes part of the fabric itself. It is the method I used for the projects in this book.

2. Use <u>only</u> Crayola brand crayons. Other brands can be waxy and less vibrant. Do not use washable crayons.

3. Choose 100% cotton for your fabric. The weave or texture of the fabric will directly affect the way the crayon looks when it is applied. I like to use tightly woven muslin or broadcloth to get a smooth finish.

4. Use a smooth surface workplace when coloring your fabric. The texture of the surface will also affect the way the crayon-colored design looks.

5. Fabric should be colored *before* you embroider. You can add some highlighting or touch up after stitching, but the base colors should always go down first.

6. You can use a Micron or Frixion pen to transfer the embroidery design to your fabric. Micron ink is permanent, so it doesn't allow for mistakes. Frixion ink allows for mistakes, but because it's heat sensitive, the design has to be traced onto your fabric more than once.

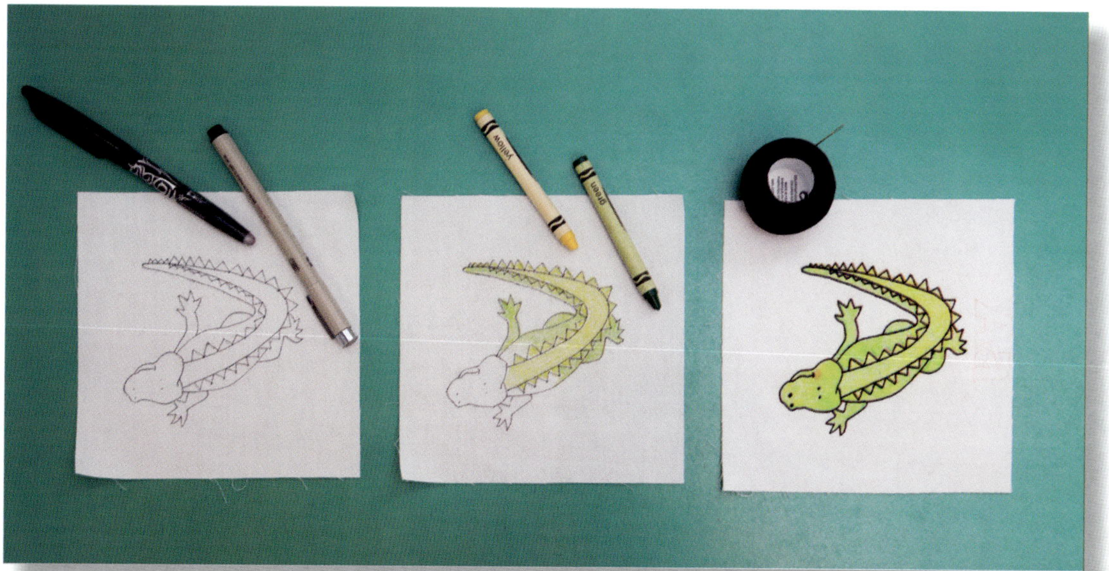

7. Some fabric artists suggest that you put down a foundation layer of white crayon before adding other colors, but I prefer to put my color directly onto the fabric. I use small circular or short straight strokes with a light touch, adding more color as I go until I reach the shade I want. Use caution when using black crayon as it seems to smear easily.

8. Be aware that the crayon cannot be erased or washed out of your fabric. It's okay to color a little past the lines.

9. After coloring your fabric, place a paper towel directly over the crayon and press with a dry iron. The paper towel will absorb any excess crayon.

10. Your artwork will probably look like a bowl of melted tutti-frutti ice cream after it's pressed, but hang in there. I've often looked at a project at this point and wondered if I'd made a mistake, but after it is embroidered, it looks beautiful.

11. You may need to color and press again to achieve the results you are looking for.

12. Back your artwork with muslin and embroider.

BEAR

In 1962, a young brown bear was flown on a B58 bomber to 35,000 feet, then was ejected from the bomber in a specially made capsule. She landed safely and became the first living creature to survive a parachute jump from a plane flying faster than sound.

CHICKEN

The greatest number of yolks ever found in a single chicken egg was nine.

DOG

In celebration of the American Kennel Club's 125th anniversary in 2009, a ranking of the top dogs in popular culture was created. Snoopy topped the list.

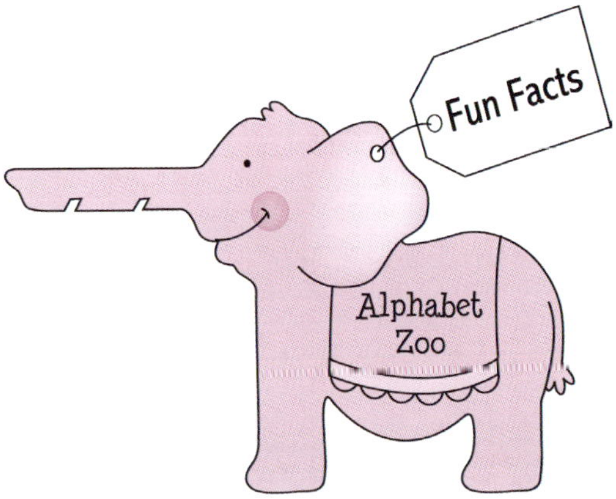

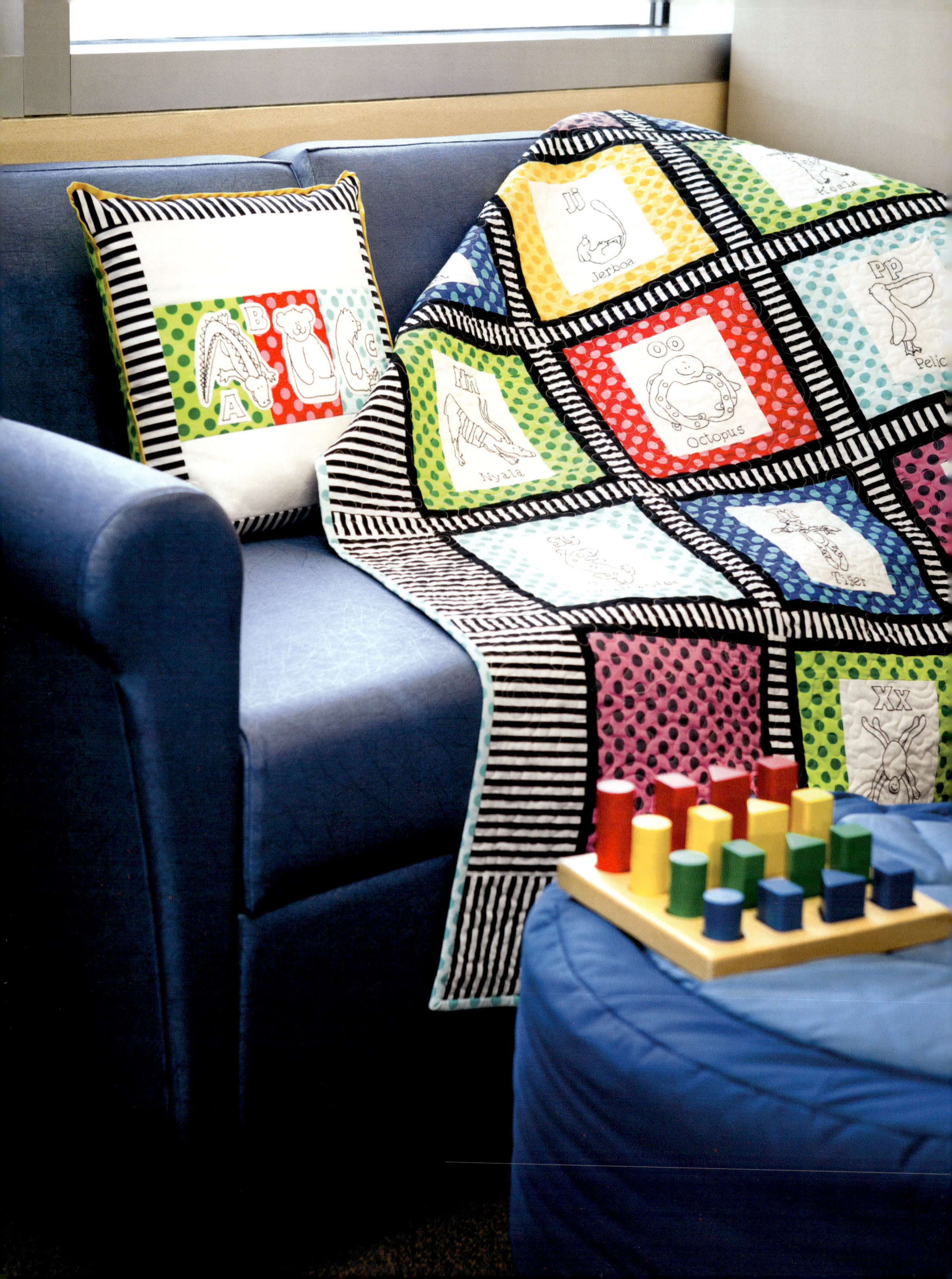

Jerboa
Koala
Octopus
Nyala
Tiger
Xx

Alphabet Zoo Quilt

No need to visit the zoo to see an elephant—there's one right here. There is also a lion, a tiger and a bear, oh my!

My favorite animal at the Woodland Park Zoo in Seattle was the tapir, but a tiger makes a better letter T. I've also included a nyala, a zorilla and a jerboa, real animals, which, like all of the animals here are shaped like the letter they represent. Any child will have fun learning their alphabet while cuddled beneath this vivid quilt.

Finished quilt measures 58" x 68"
Block size: 5" x 6 1/2"
Quilted by Terry Tamaki

FABRIC AND SUPPLIES

- Berry (red), Sunny (yellow), Grass (green), Cobalt (blue) and Peony (purple) polka dot: 1/3 yard each
- Sea (light blue) polka dot: 1 yard
- Solid black: 1 yard
- Clown Stripe White: 2 yards
- Solid white: 2 1/2 yards
- Muslin (optional for backing embroidery): 2 1/2 yards
- Backing: 4 yards
- Batting (90" wide): 2 yards
- Embroidery floss: DMC Perle Cotton size 12 in Black (#310)
- 5" or 7" embroidery hoop
- Embroidery needle size 8
- Pigma pen or Frixion pen for tracing

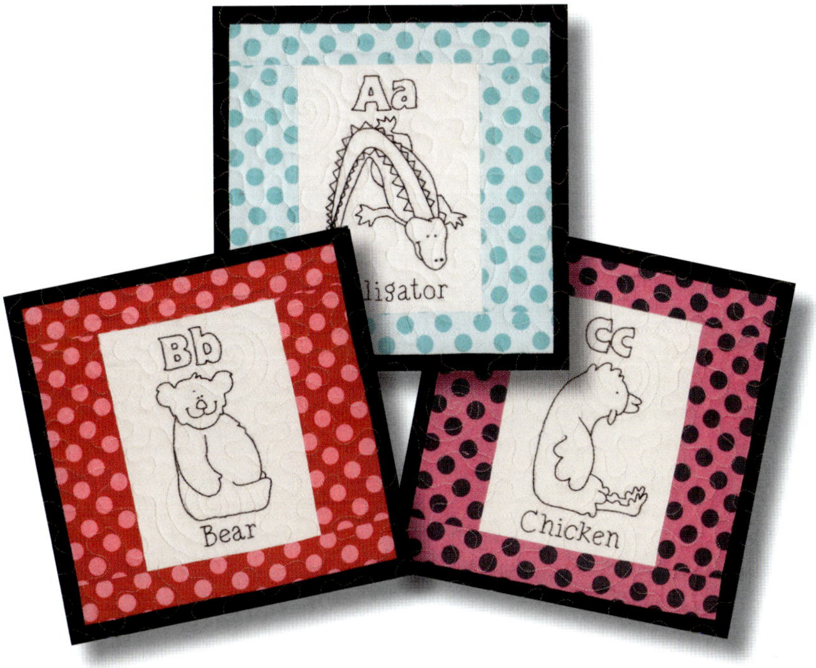

Alphabet Zoo Quilt continued

CUTTING INSTRUCTIONS

Pre-wash all fabric before cutting. Instructions include a 1/4″ seam allowance except where noted.

Solid White *and* Muslin: 26 – 9″ squares of each (will be trimmed after embroidery)

Berry:
- 10 – 2 1/4″ x 6 1/2″ strips
- 10 – 1 1/2″ x 8 1/2″ strips

Sunny, Cobalt, Peony and Grass:
- 8 – 2 1/4″ x 6 1/2″ strips of each
- 8 – 1 1/2″ x 8 1/2″ strips of each
- 1 – 8 1/2″ x 8 1/2″ square of each

Sea:
- 10 – 2 1/4″ x 6 1/2″
- 10 – 1 1/2″ x 8 1/2″
- 7 – 2 1/4″ x width of fabric for binding

Solid Black:
- 60 – 1″ x 8 1/2″
- 60 – 1″ x 9 1/2″

Clown Stripe White:

Cut fabric so stripes are perpendicular to the long edge.
- 24 – 1 1/2″ x 9 1/2″ strips for sashing
- 5 – 1 1/2″ x 58 1/2″strips for sashing
- 12 – 5″ x 9 1/2″ strips for border
- 2 – 5″ x 58 1/2″ strips for border (may need to be pieced)

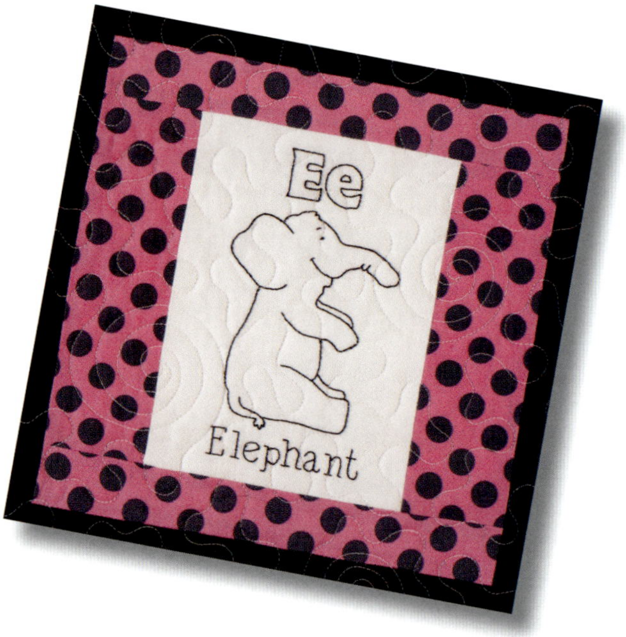

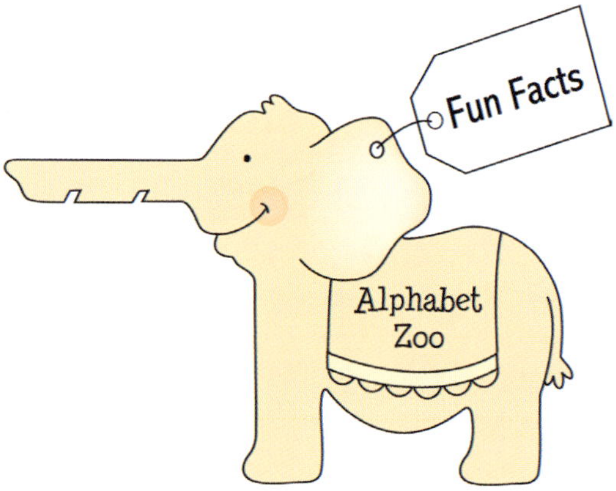

ELEPHANT

Because elephants need to spend a great deal of time eating to support their large size, they normally sleep only two or three hours each day.

ASSEMBLY

- Embroider 26 alphabet blocks. Trim individual blocks to 5″ wide x 6 1/2″ high, making certain that alphabet letters are centered.

- <u>*For the 4 corner blocks:*</u> stitch a solid black 1″ x 8 1/2″ strip to each side of an 8 1/2″ square polka-dot block, then stitch a 1″ x 9 1/2″ solid black strip to the top and bottom. Press and square up all 4 blocks.

- <u>*For the 26 animal blocks:*</u> Using the guide below, stitch a 2 1/4″ x 6 1/2″ polka-dot strip to each side of the trimmed animal blocks, then stitch a 1 1/2″ x 8 1/2″ strip to the top and bottom.
  Sea (light blue): Alligator, Hare, Pelican, Salamander and Zorilla
  Berry (red): Bear, Dog, Lion, Octopus and Worm
  Peony (purple): Chicken, Elephant, Moose and Unicorn
  Cobalt (blue): Fox, Insect, Quail and Tiger
  Sunny (yellow): Gorilla, Jerboa, Rooster and Yabby
  Grass (green): Koala, Nyala, Vampire bat and Xysticus ulmi

- Stitch a solid black 1″ x 8 1/2″ strip to the sides of each polka-dot block. Stitch a 1″ x 9 1/2″ strips to the top and bottom of each block. Press and square up the blocks.

- Beginning with the top row of blocks, stitch a 5″ x 9 1/2″ striped fabric strip to the **left**-hand edge of a yellow polka-dot block. Stripes will be <u>horizontal</u>. Add the alligator, bear and chicken blocks to the row, using the 1 1/2″ x 9″ horizontally-striped sashing strips between each block. End the top row by stitching another 5″ x 9 1/2″ striped fabric strip to the right-hand edge of the green polka-dot block.

- Construct the remaining rows in the same manner, following the photograph on page 19.

- Stitch the rows together with a 1 1/2″ x 58″ strip of striped sashing between each row. Stripes will be <u>vertical</u>. Add a 5″ x 58″ vertically-striped border to the top and the bottom of quilt.

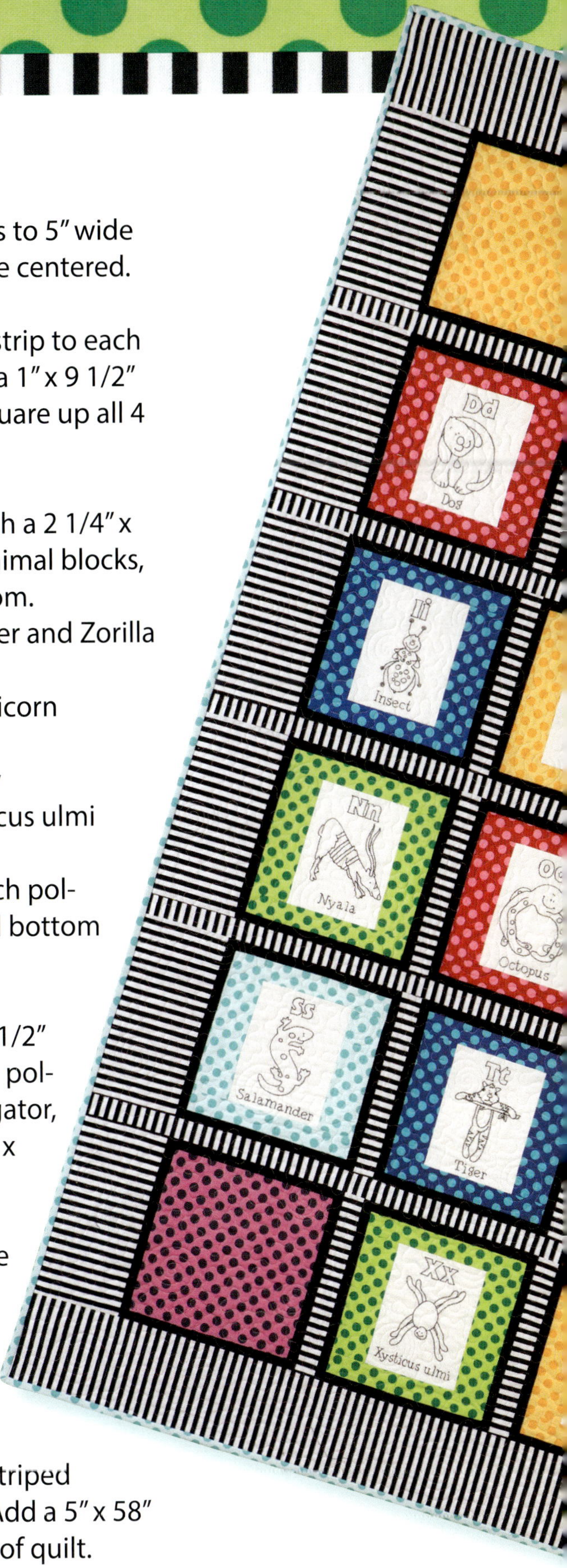

Alphabet Zoo Quilt continued

FINISHING

Quilt as desired, trim excess backing and batting, square your quilt and then bind.

QUILTING SUGGESTIONS

Simple geometric designs that do not overpower the impact of the blackwork are the best choices to use for the borders, or as an overall pattern for this quilt. The blackwork blocks may be stitched in the ditch around the outer edges, and the centers quilted with an overall wavy crosshatch grid pattern. Echo quilting the embroidery is another good option.

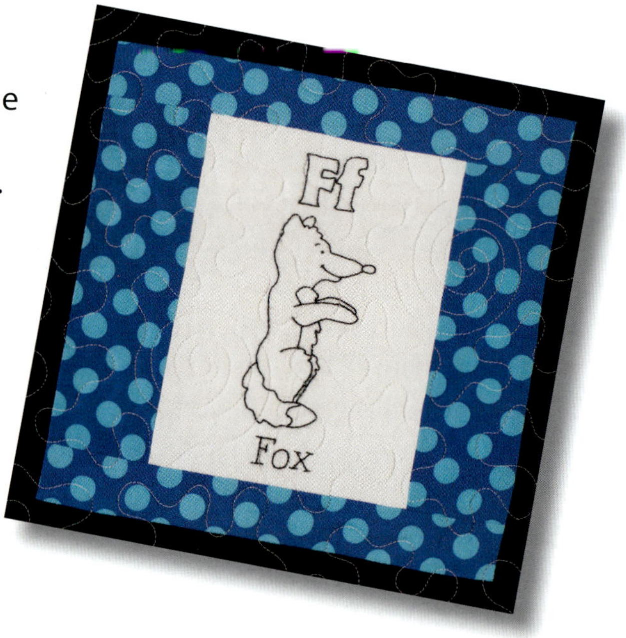

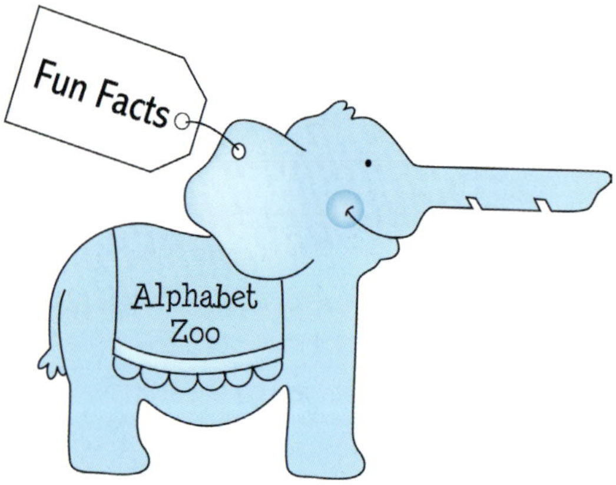

FOX

Foxes are often characterized in popular folklore as tricky or cunning creatures, sometimes having magical powers.

GORILLA

"King Kong" is rated #12 on the American Film Institute's top 100 Thrills list.

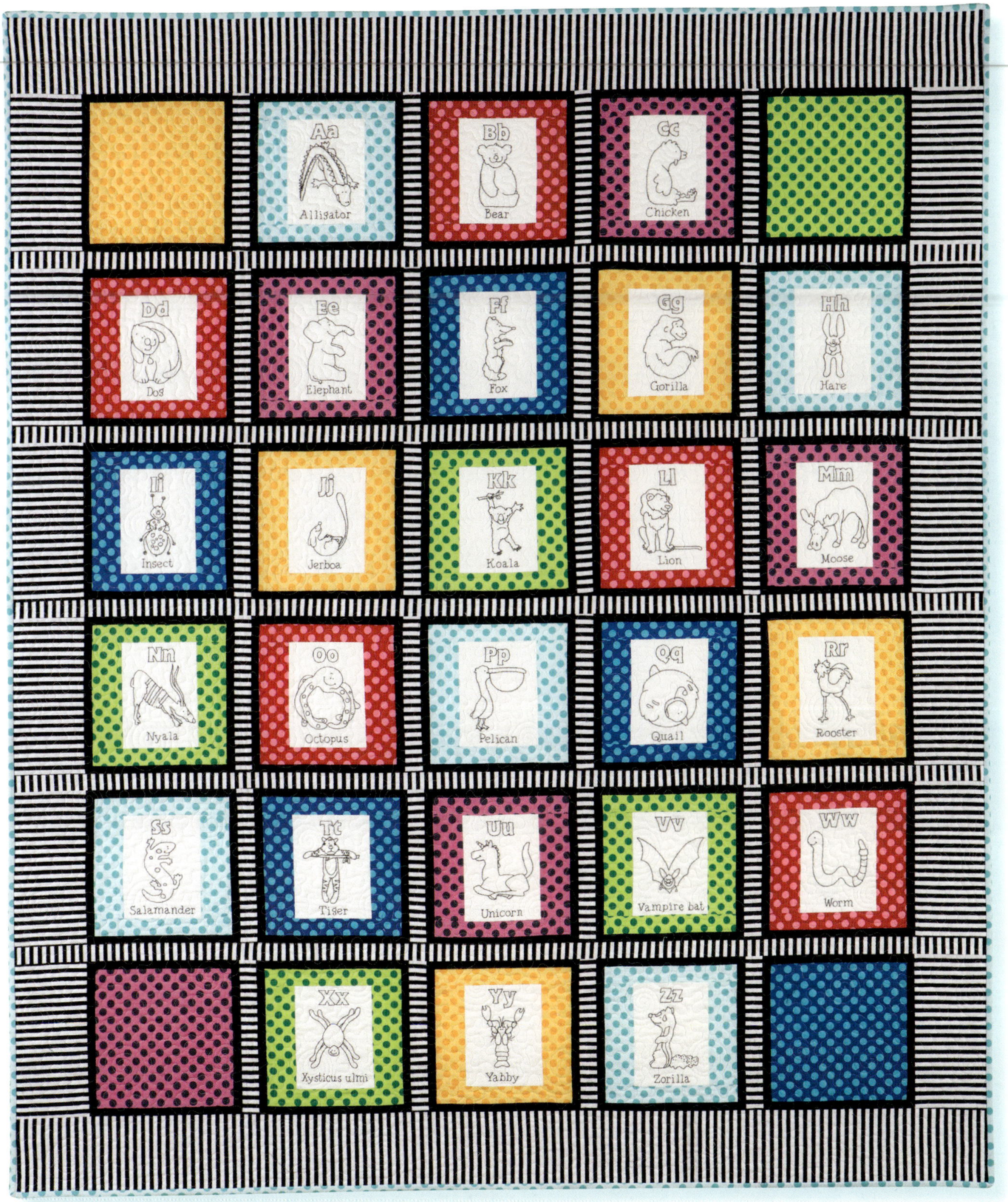
Aa
Alligator
Bb
Bear
Cc
Chicken
Dd
Dog
Ee
Elephant
Ff
Fox
Gg
Gorilla
Hh
Hare
Ii
Insect
Jj
Jerboa
Kk
Koala
Ll
Lion
Mm
Moose
Nn
Nyala
Oo
Octopus
Pp
Pelican
Qq
Quail
Rr
Rooster
Ss
Salamander
Tt
Tiger
Uu
Unicorn
Vv
Vampire bat
Ww
Worm
Xx
Xysticus ulmi
Yy
Yabby
Zz
Zorilla

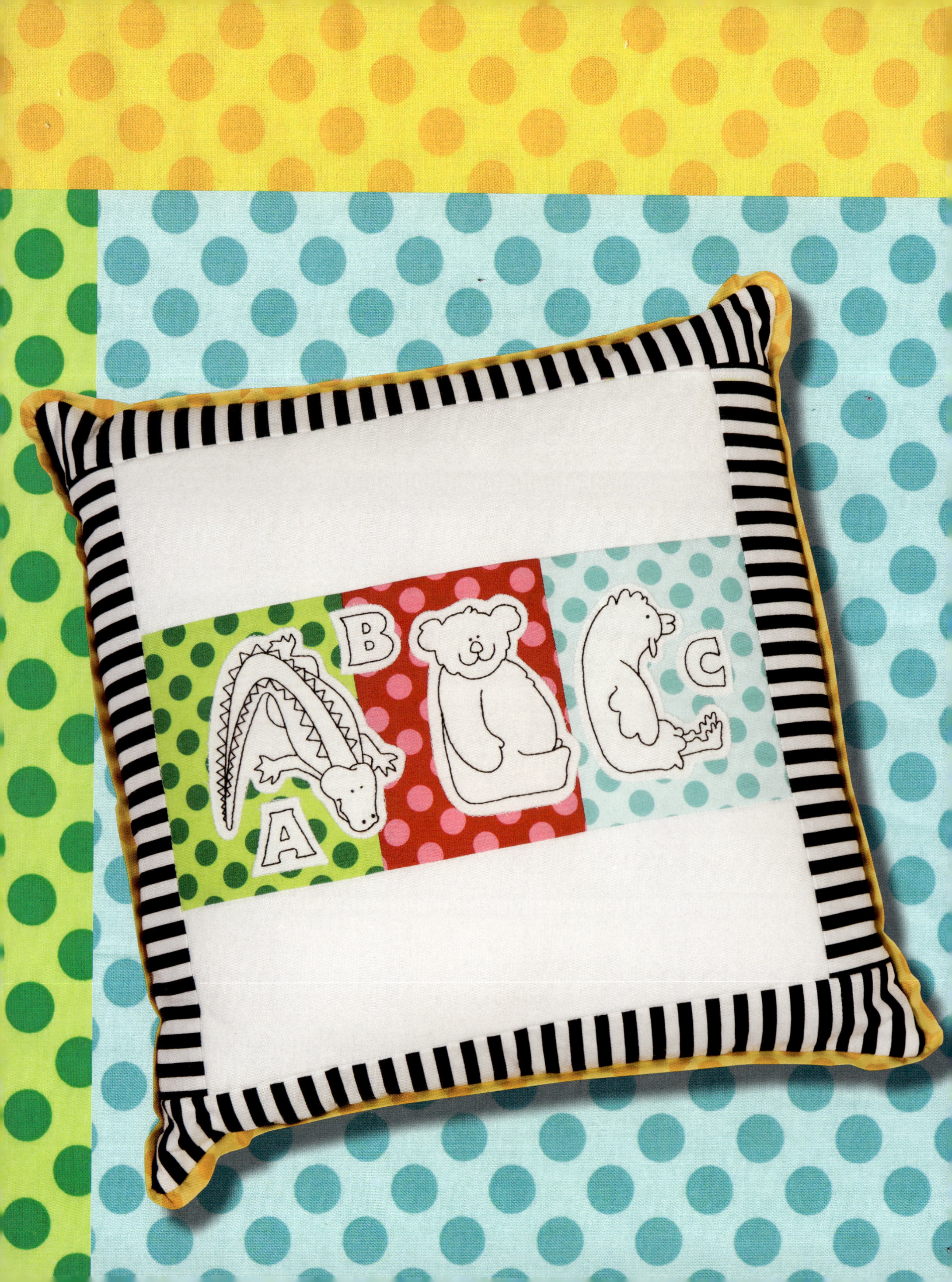
B
C
A

ABC Pillow

Making this pillow is as easy as A, B, C and is the perfect complement to the Alphabet Zoo quilt.

Finished pillow measures 14" square, not including trim.

FABRIC AND SUPPLIES

- Solid white: 1/4 yard
- Muslin: 1/4 yard for backing embroidery
- Berry (red), and Sea (light blue): 6" square of each
- Sunny (yellow): 1/8 yard
- Grass (green): 1/4 yard
- Clown Stripe White (black and white stripe): 1/8 yard
- Batting (optional): 14 1/2" square
- Double-sided fusible webbing: 1/2 yard
- 14" zipper
- 14" x 14" pillow form
- Embroidery floss: DMC Perle Cotton size 12 in #310 Black
- 5" or 7" embroidery hoop
- Embroidery needle size 8
- Pigma pen or Frixion pen
- Fabric glue or Fray Check (optional)

HARE

In 1987, Greece issued a 130 drachma postage stamp that featured an illustration of Aesop's "Tortoise and the Hare" fable.

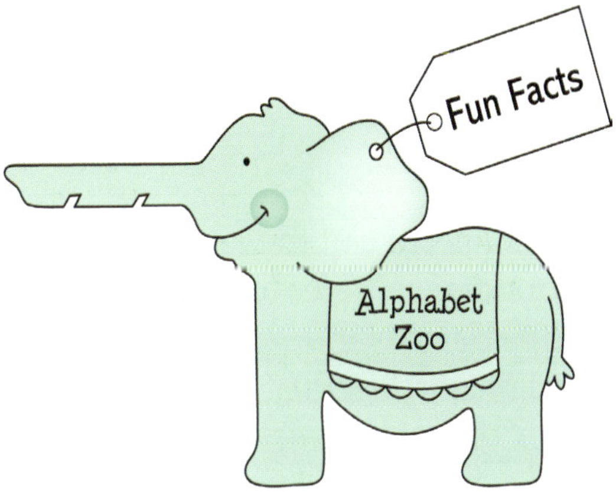

ABC Pillow continued

CUTTING INSTRUCTIONS

Solid white:

- 2 – 3 3/8″ x 11″ strips
- 3 – 6″ squares (or 1 strip approximately 18″ x 6″) for embroidery

Muslin:

- 3 – 6″ squares (or 1 strip approximately 18″ x 6″) for backing the embroidery

Fusible webbing:

- 3 – 6″ squares (or 1 strip approximately 18″ x 6″)

Berry:

- 1 – 4″ x 5 1/4″ block

Sunny:

- 1 – 1 1/4″ x approximately 60″ long strip for the trim

Sea:

- 1 – 4 x 5 1/4″ block

Grass:

- 1 – 4 x 5 1/4″ block
- 2 – 7 3/4″ x 14 1/2″ strips

Clown Stripe White:

- 2 – 2 1/4″ x 14 1/2″ strips
- 2 – 2 1/4″ x 11″ strips

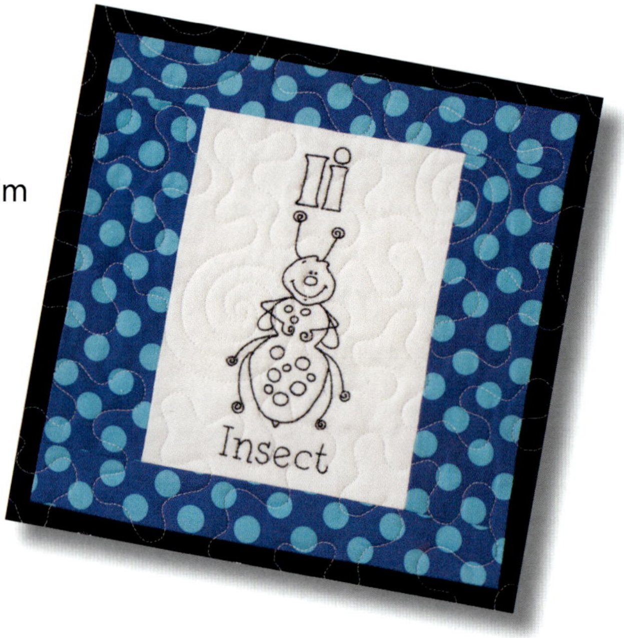

ASSEMBLY

Embroidery

- Transfer capital letters A, B and C, plus an alligator, bear and chicken from the Alphabet Zoo templates on pages 57-73 onto the solid white fabric. Back the fabric with muslin and embroider following the General Instructions on page 8.

- Fuse the webbing to the back of the embroidered pieces.

- Carefully cut out the animals and letters, leaving a 1/4″ border around each (refer to the photo as a guide). You may want to use a tiny dab of fabric glue or Fray Check between the white solid and muslin layers of the cutouts to keep them from fraying.

PILLOW FRONT

- With long sides matching and right sides together, stitch Grass, Berry and Sea blocks into a long strip, with the Berry block in the middle. Refer to the photo to determine placement of the animals and letters. Fuse and appliqué to the polka-dotted blocks using your favorite appliqué stitch.

- Sew a 3 3/8″ x 11″ white solid strip to the top and bottom of the polka-dot block strip. Sew a 2 1/4″ x 11″ Clown Stripe White strip to each side of the block. Sew a 2 1/4″ x 14 1/2″ strip to the top and bottom to complete the pillow front.

- Place the pillow front on top of the 14 1/2″ square of batting and stitch in the ditch around the polka-dot strip and borders to hold them in place. This step is optional, but will create a smooth, finished look for your pillow.

- Fold the yellow strip in half lengthwise. Pin to the edge of the pillow front, matching raw edges. Baste, gathering the yellow strip slightly when easing around the corners.

PILLOW BACK

- Sew the long edges of the 7 3/4″ x 14 1/2″ Grass strips, right sides together, with a 1/2″ seam.

- Install the zipper according to the instructions included with the zipper. Leave about 1″ at each end of the seam closed to cover the zipper ends.

FINISHING

- Stitch pillow back to pillow front, right sides together.

- Turn right sides out. Press and insert pillow form.

INSECT

The average worker bee produces only 1/12 teaspoon of honey in its entire insect lifetime.

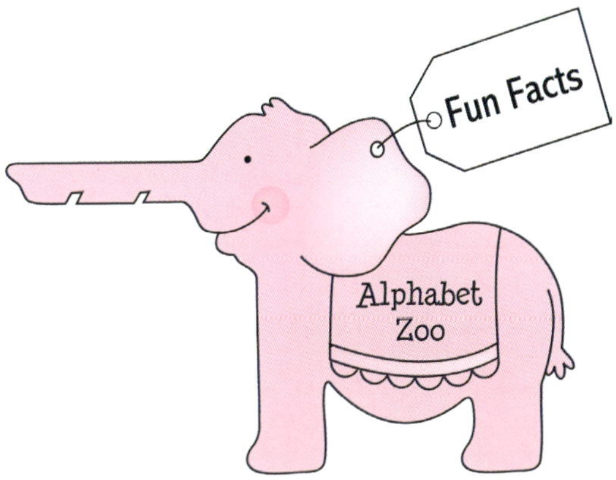

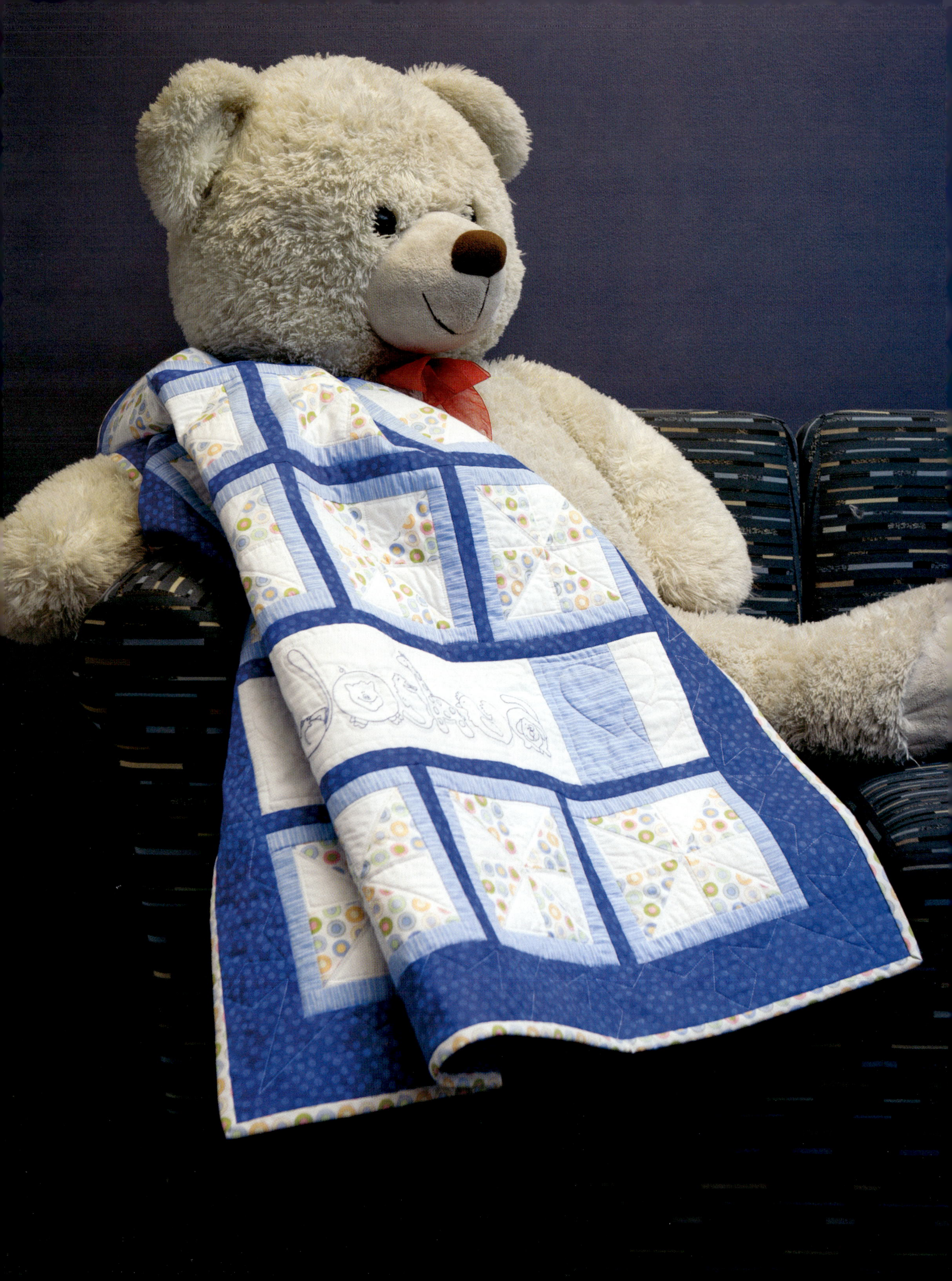

Joshua Pinwheel Quilt

Personalization puts a fun spin on the traditional pinwheel quilt.

The Pinwheel pattern is one of my favorites. It's cheerful, but simple – a perfect choice for this quilt that features a child's name stitched in Alphabet Zoo animals. Depending on the length of the name, you can add a solid white block to the name row and add a birthdate, birth statistics or a short message.

Finished quilt measures 34" x 41"

FABRIC AND SUPPLIES

- White solid: 5/8 yard
- Muslin (optional): 1/4 yard for backing embroidery
- Multi-color polka dot: 5/8 yard
- Light blue stripe: 1/2 yard
- Medium blue polka dot: 1 yard
- Binding: 1/3 yard
- Batting (90" wide): 1 1/3 yards
- Backing: 1 1/3 yards
- Embroidery floss: DMC #798 Dark Delft Blue, or the color of your choice
- 5" or 7" embroidery hoop
- Embroidery needle size 8
- Pigma pen or Frixion pen

JERBOA

The Jerboa is a desert rodent with hind legs about four times longer than its forelimbs. This allows the jerboa to hop like a kangaroo.

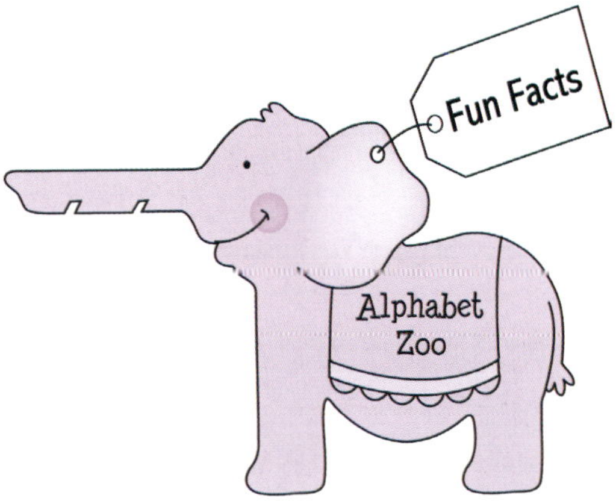

Joshua Pinwheel Quilt continued

CUTTING INSTRUCTIONS

White solid:

- 1 – 8″ x length of name plus 5″ (the 5″ is for ease in working with embroidery hoop)
- 32 – 3 3/8″ squares for the pinwheels

Muslin:

- 1 – 8″ high x length of name plus 5″ strip for backing the embroidery

Multi-colored polka dots:

- 32 – 3 3/8″ squares for the pinwheels
- 4 – 2 1/4″ x WOF for binding

Light blue stripe:

- 32 – 1 1/4″ x 5 1/2″ strips
- 32 – 1 1/4″ x 7″ strips

Medium blue polka dots:

- 13 – 1 1/4″ x 7″ strips for vertical sashing
- 4 – 1 1/4″ x 24 1/4" strips for horizontal sashing
- 4 – 3 1/2″ x 34 3/4″ strips for border

ASSEMBLY

Half-square Triangle Units

- Place a white 3 3/8″ square on top of a multi-colored polka-dot 3 3/8″ square, right sides together. Draw a line diagonally from one corner to the opposite corner. Stitch 1/4" on each side of the drawn line. Cut on the diagonal line. Open, trim the dog ears and press toward darker color. Repeat for the remainder of the 3 3/8″ sets. You will have 64 white/multi-colored squares when you are finished.

- Sew 2 half-square triangle blocks together as shown in Diagram 1.

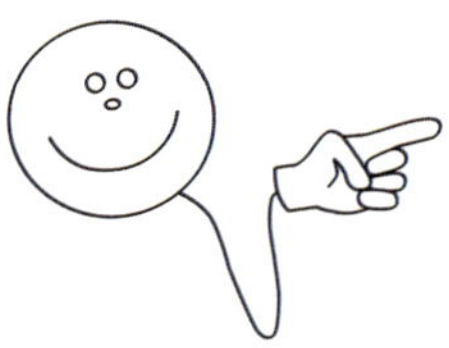

TIP: *Spraying the squares with starch before pressing will help prevent the bias from stretching.*

DIAGRAM 1

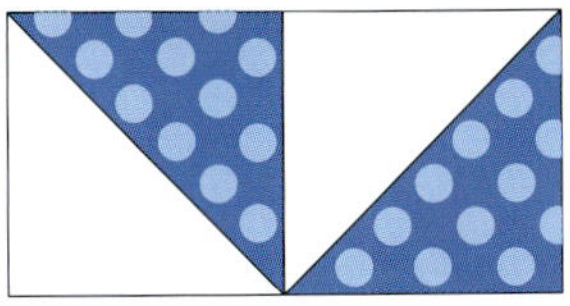

- Assemble the squares according to Diagram 2 to create 16 – 5 1/2″ square pinwheel blocks.

DIAGRAM 2

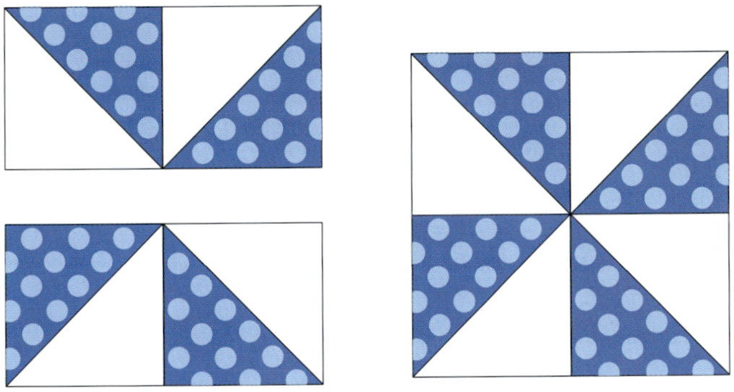

- Sew a 1 1/4″ x 5 3/4″ x blue stripe strip to each side of the pinwheel squares.
- Sew a 1 1/4″ x 7″ strip to the top and bottom of each pinwheel square.

ASSEMBLE THE ROWS

- Make a row of 4 pinwheel blocks by stitching a 7″ x 1 1/4″ blue polka-dot strip between the blocks (see photograph). Make 4 rows of 4 blocks each.

- Stitch 3 rows together with a 1 1/4″ x 24 1/4" blue polka-dot sashing strip between each row. The fourth row will be added later.

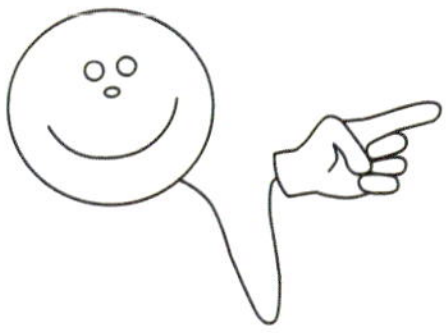

TIP: *It is especially important with this project to trace or photocopy the name onto a sheet of paper before you transfer it to your fabric to make sure the letters are spaced correctly.*

Joshua Pinwheel Quilt Continued

- Embroider the name on white fabric backed with muslin (see General Instructions page 10). Center the name vertically and trim the block to 5 3/4" high. The lower edge of the name should be approximately 1 1/4" from the lower edge of the fabric.

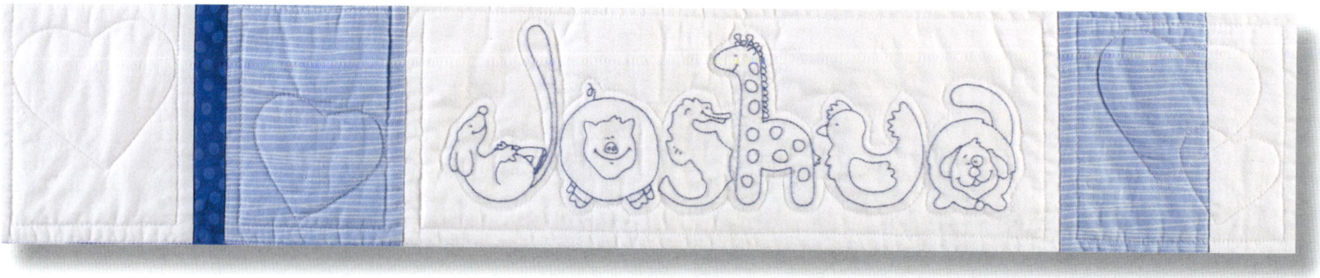

- Trim the length of the block, centering the name horizontally and adding about 1" on each side of the name. Referring to the photograph on page 29, add two 5 3/4" high pieces of light blue stripe, the remaining 1 1/4" x 5 3/4" blue polka dot-strip and two 5 3/4" high white solid piece 28 3/4" strip.

- Add a 1 1/4" x 28 3/4" strip of blue polka dot to the top and bottom of the name row.

- Stitch a single pinwheel row to the bottom of the name row.

- Stitch the 3-row pinwheel set to the top of the name row.

- Stitch a border strip to each side of quilt, and then to the top and bottom.

FINISHING

- Quilt as desired and bind.

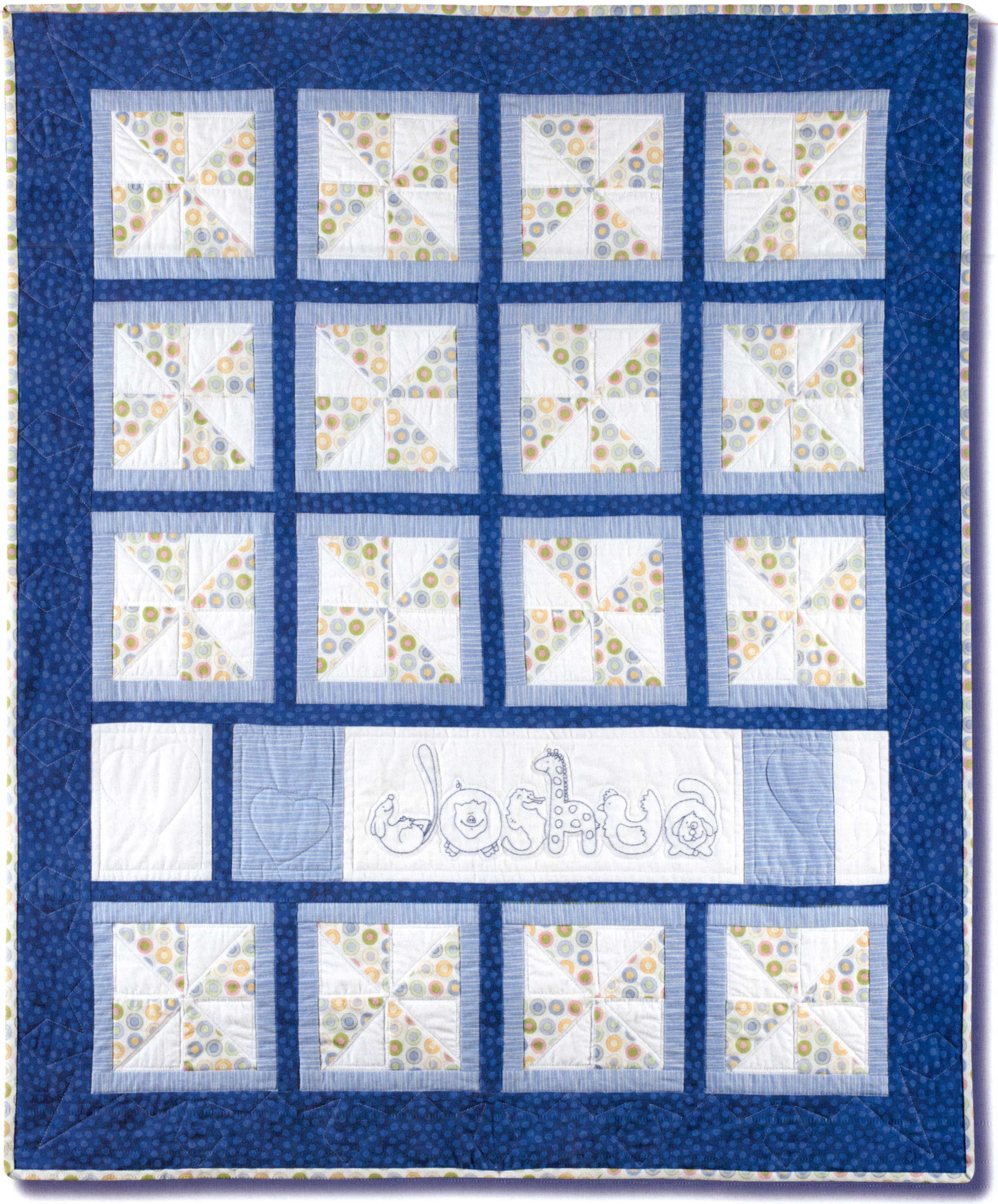
Joshua

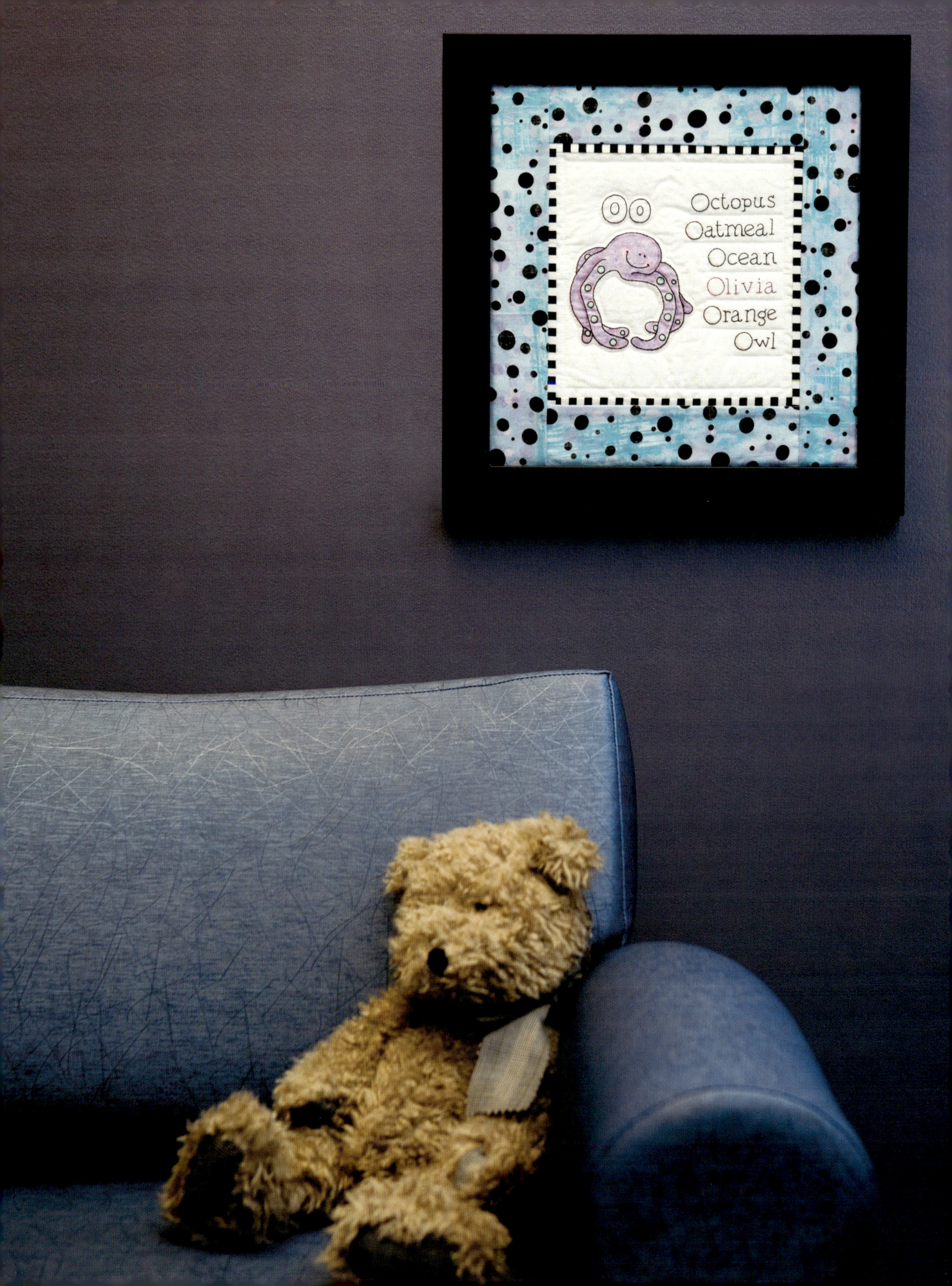
Oo
Octopus
Oatmeal
Ocean
Olivia
Orange
Owl

O is for Olivia

A letter-perfect quilt block!

This block is a quick project that makes a terrific shower or birthday gift. It reminds me of that old jump rope rhyme, "A my name is Alice … " where each verse is full of words that start with the different letters of the alphabet. A complete alphabet is provided on page 74 to create your own words.

Finished project measures 12 1/2" square

FABRIC AND SUPPLIES

- White: 1 fat quarter
- Muslin: 12" square for backing embroidery
- Blue print: 1/4 yard
- Clown Stripe White: 1/8 yard
- Batting: 12 1/2" square Warm and White or similar type low-loft cotton batting
- Lightweight foam core: 12" square
- Repositionable spray adhesive
- Picture frame with 12" x 12" opening (sample uses frame with 1 1/2" borders)
- DMC Perle Cotton size 12 in #310 Black
- 2 strands of bright-colored embroidery floss for the name
- Crayola crayons

KOALA

Other than primates, the koala is one of the few mammals that have distinctive fingerprints.

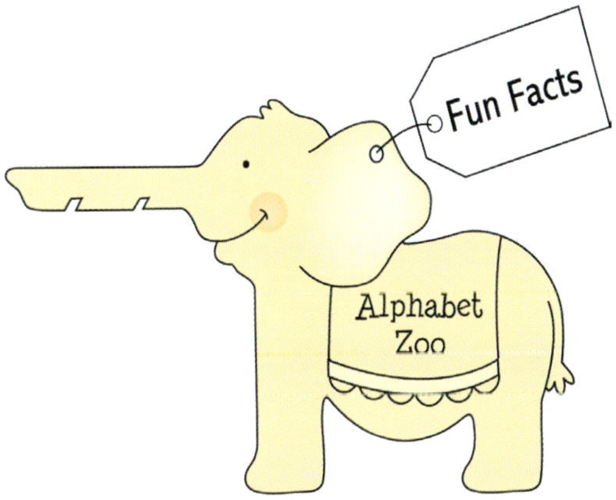

O is for Olivia continued

CUTTING INSTRUCTIONS

White:

- 1 – 10 1/2″ square

Muslin:

- 1 – 10 1/2″ square

Blue print:

- 2 – 2 1/2″ x 12 1/2″ strips for side borders
- 2 – 2 1/2″ x 8 1/2″ strips for top and bottom borders

Clown Stripe White:

- 4 – 1″ x 8 1/2″ strips

ASSEMBLY

- Refer to the instructions on how to color fabric with crayons on page 12. Using the "Olivia Octopus" template on page 74 as a guide, trace and color the animal letter of your choice onto the 10 1/2″ white square. Trace the child's name and five words that start with the same letter onto the white fabric using the letter patterns and template on page 74.

- Following the General Instructions for embroidery on page 10, layer the crayoned block with the 10 1/2″ muslin square.

- Embroider the animal letter and word lettering with black floss.

- Embroider child's name with colored floss that complements the animal.

- Center and trim the finished block to 8 1/2″ square.

- Fold the strips of black and white striped fabric in half lengthwise to create a flange. Pin the flange sections to the top and bottom edges of the embroidered block, raw edges together. Stitch with a 1/4″ seam. Stitch a flange to each side of the square.

- Add the borders to the block by stitching a 2 1/2″ x 8 1/2″ blue print strip to both the top and bottom and a 2 1/2″ x 12 1/2″ strip to each side. Square the block.

FINISHING

- Place a layer of batting on the back of the completed block. If you wish to quilt the block, do so now.

- Open the back of the frame and remove the glass. Use spray adhesive to adhere the finished block to the 12 1/2" square of foam core. Reassemble the frame without the glass, trimming the foam core with a rotary cutter if necessary for a good fit.

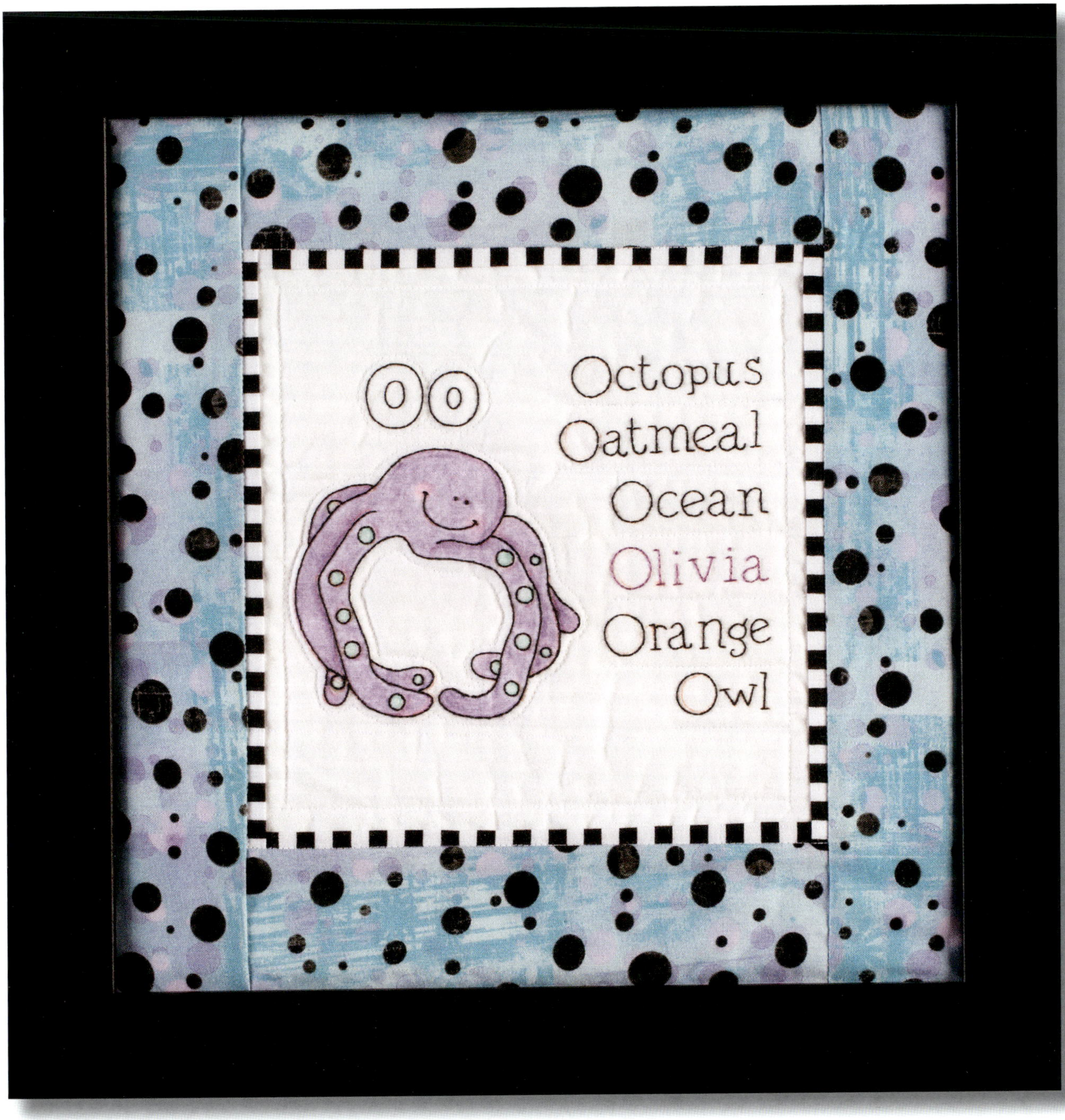

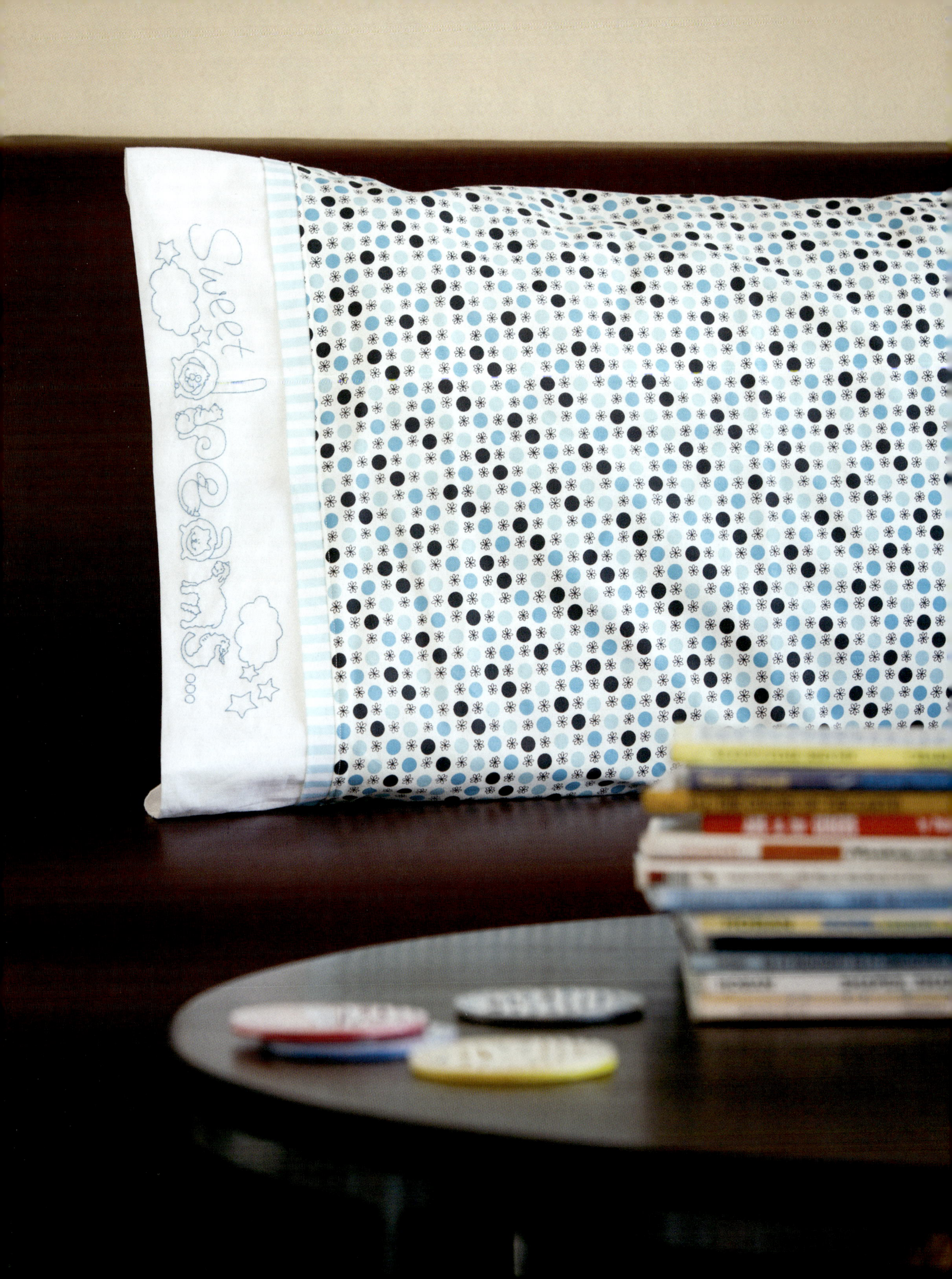
Sweet Dreams...

Sweet Dreams

You'll be counting sheep – as well as kittens and puppies – when you lay your head down on this pretty pillowcase.

There is more than one way to construct a pillowcase. I like the "burrito" or "magic" method because it's quick, and it eliminates the need to hand stitch your cuff down to the inside of the case. This method has become quite popular and tutorials can easily be found on the Internet.

Finished pillowcase measures 21″ x 32″
Embroidery design: page 75

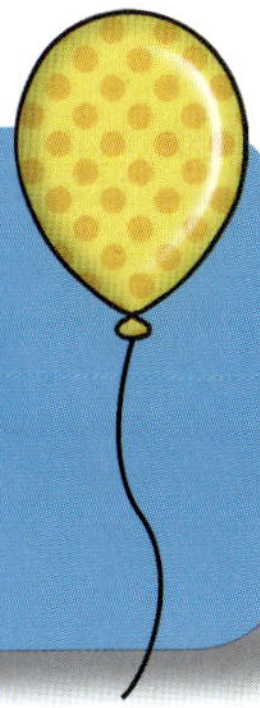

FABRIC AND SUPPLIES

- White solid: 1/3 yard for embroidered cuff
- Blue polka dot: 7/8 yard (main fabric)
- Blue and white stripe: 1/8 yard for trim
- Embroidery floss: DMC #3760 Medium Wedgewood Blue (or the color of your choice)
- 5″ or 7″ embroidery hoop
- Embroidery needle size 8
- Pigma pen or Frixion pen

CUTTING INSTRUCTIONS

White solid:
- 1 – 9″ x 42″ rectangle

Blue polka dot:
- 1 – 28″ x 42″ rectangle

Blue and white stripe:
- 1 – 1″ x 42″ strip

LION
If you want to estimate a lion's age, take a good look at his mane. The darker the mane, the older the lion.

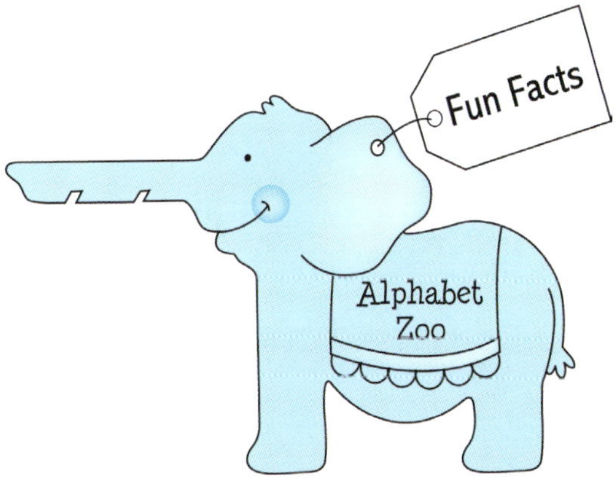

Sweet Dreams continued

EMBROIDERY

- Begin by folding and pressing the white 9" x 42" rectangle in half lengthwise to determine the front and back of the cuff. Now fold and press the strip in half widthwise. The strip should now have 4 "section" creases – 2 rows of 2 rectangles.

- Place the sectioned strip on a work surface, right side up. Center and trace the embroidery pattern onto the upper left quarter/rectangle.

- Following the General Embroidery instructions on page 10, embroider the design. Make sure you are embroidering it on a single layer of fabric.

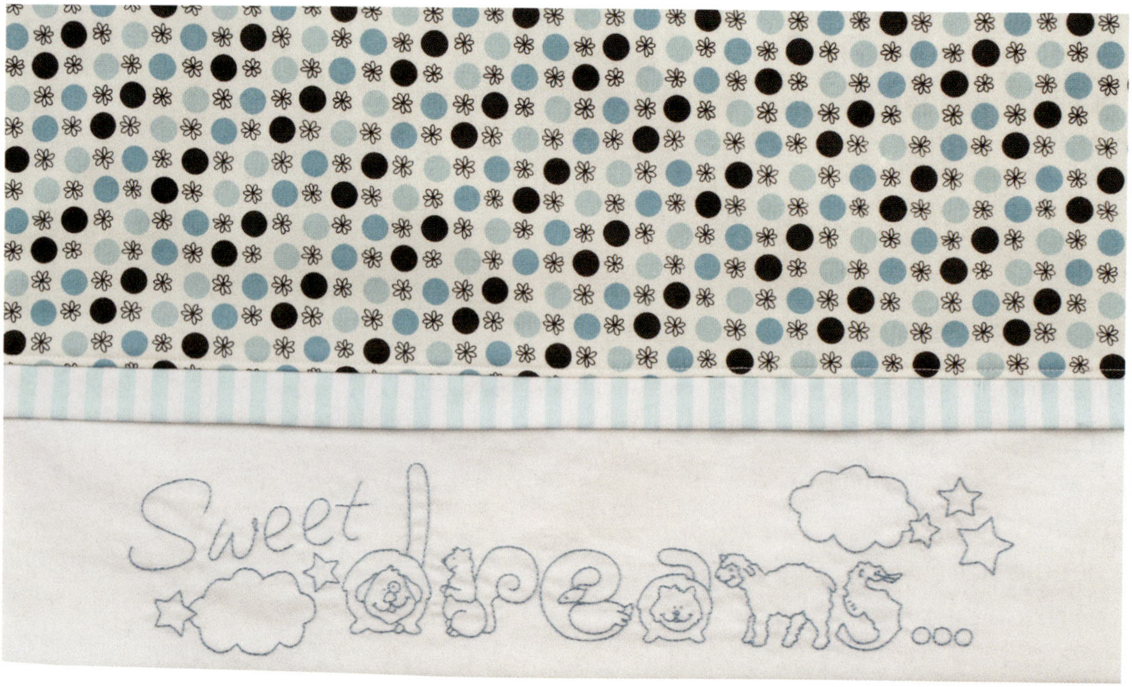

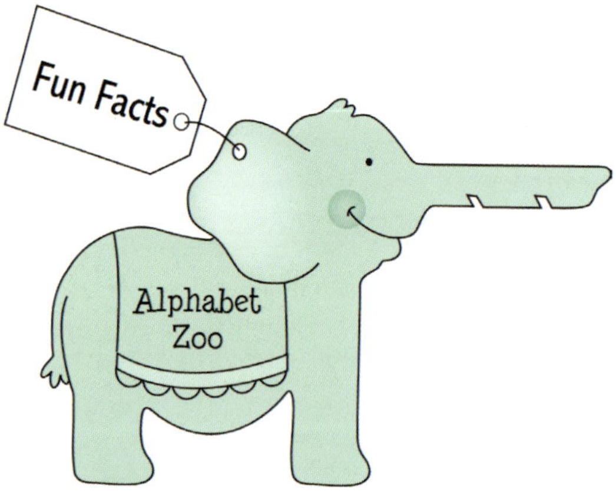

MOOSE

Male moose shed their antlers every winter and grow back a larger set the next spring.

ASSEMBLY

- The pillowcase is made using a popular method called the "burrito" pillowcase. Many images and examples of this method can be found on the Internet if needed.

- Fold trim strip in half lengthwise.

- Lay the embroidered cuff out flat on your work surface, right side up, with the embroidery at the upper left.

- Place the folded trim on top of the cuff, aligning the raw edges.

- Position the blue polka dot on top of the trim, right side facing down, and the top edges aligned. You now have 3 layers – cuff, trim and main fabric. The cuff and main fabric are right sides together with the trim in between.

- Baste the layers together.

- Starting with the bottom edge, roll the polka-dot fabric up until it reaches about the midpoint of the cuff.

- Bring the bottom edge of the cuff up over the roll (encasing the roll), and match it to the top raw edges to create a tube.

- Pin and stich 1/4" from the raw edges through all three layers.

- To turn right side out, pull the print fabric from inside one end of the tube until everything is unfolded and laying flat. The cuff, trim and body of the pillowcase will all be stitched together, with no need to hand sew the cuff to the inside of the case.

FINISHING

- Sew a French seam by folding the pillowcase in half lengthwise, right side out, matching raw edges. Stitch a 1/8" to scant 1/4" seam down the side of the pillowcase and across the bottom. Trim the corners.

- Turn the pillowcase so that the right sides are together and the wrong side is facing out. Press.

- Stitch another 1/4" seam down the side and across the bottom of the pillowcase, enclosing the first seam. Turn right side out and press.

NYALA

This South African antelope uses a sharp, high, dog-like bark to warn others in his troop about danger.

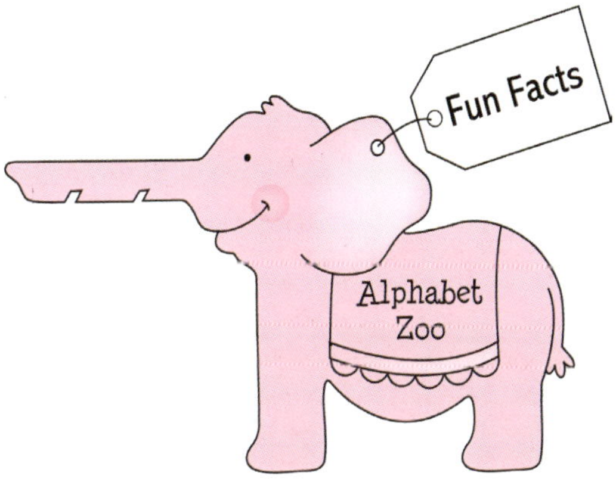

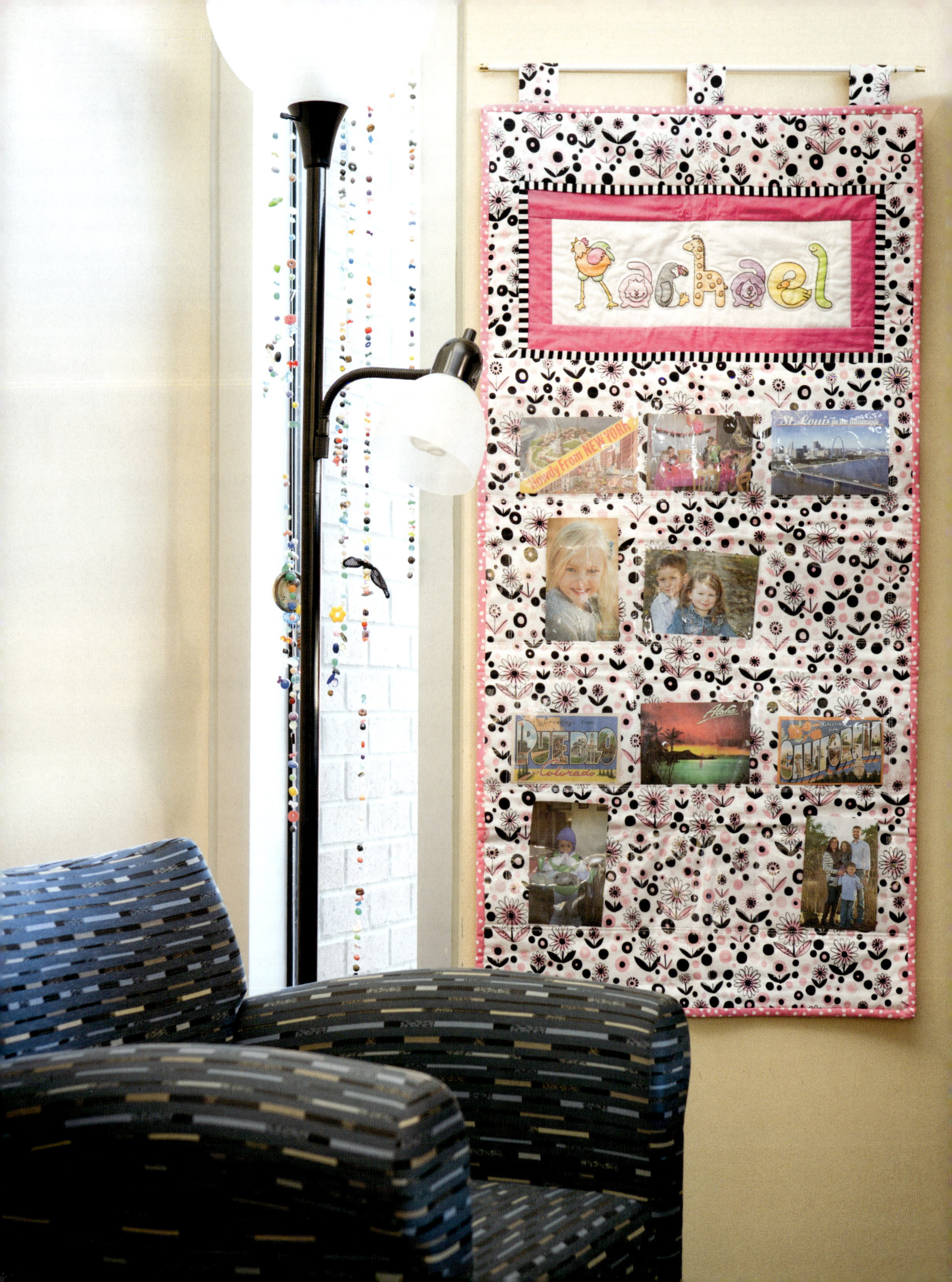
Rachael
Howdy From NEW YORK
St. Louis
PUEBLO
Colorado
Aloha
CALIFORNIA

Rachael Hanging Pockets

Wish you were here!

My young grandson, Miles, loves to take pictures. When I noticed that he was taping some of his favorite photos to the inside of his closet door, I thought it would be great if he had a better way to display them, along with postcards and small drawings he might collect. This hanging pocket banner is based on those shoe caddies that hang over the back of a door. The clear vinyl pockets protect photos and cards and make swapping them out and updating the display a snap.

Finished wall hanging measures 22 1/2" x 42 1/2"

FABRIC AND SUPPLIES

- White solid: 1/3 yard
- Muslin (optional): 1/3 yard
- Bright flower print: 1 1/4 yards
- Solid pink: 1/4 yard
- Black and white stripes: 1/8 yard
- Clear vinyl, 16 gauge (54" wide): 1/3 yard*
- Pink polka dots: 1 3/4 yards (for both binding and back)
- Binding alone: 1/4 yard
- Backing alone: 1 1/2 yards
- Batting (90" wide): 3/4 yard
- Black embroidery floss, size 12
- Embroidery needle
- Masking tape
- Crayola crayons

**Clear vinyl can usually be found in the upholstery section of your local fabric shop*

OCTOPUS

Octopuses can change color as a method of camouflage. They can also alter the texture of their skin, making detection even more difficult.

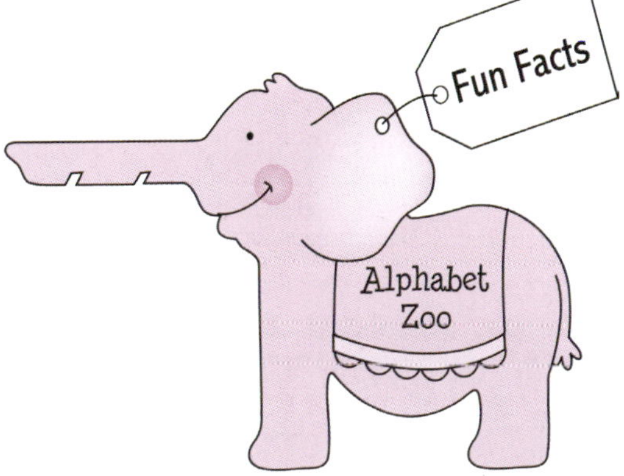

Rachael Hanging Pockets continued

CUTTING INSTRUCTIONS

White solid:

- 1 – 9″ x 18″ rectangle for embroidery

Muslin:

- 1 – 9″ x 18″ rectangle for backing embroidery

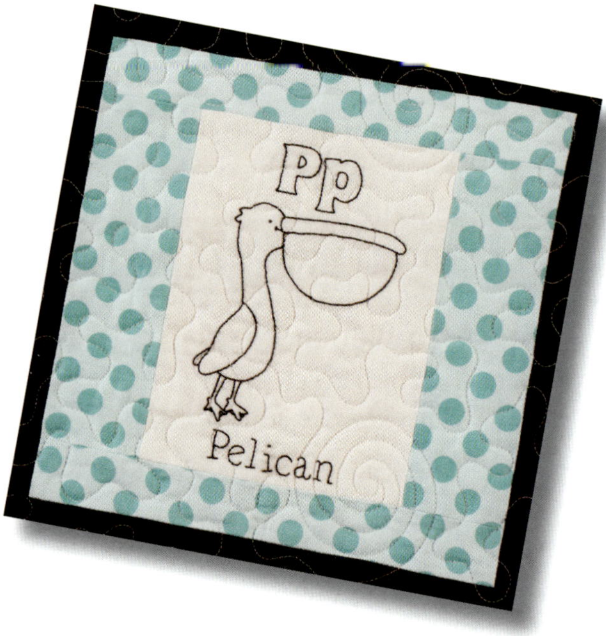

Bright flower print:

- 3 – 4 1/2″ x 5 1/2″ strips for hanging tabs
- 2 – 2″ x 9 1/4″ strips
- 1 – 4″ x 22 1/4″ strip
- 1 – 22 1/4″ x 32 1/2″ rectangle

Pink polka dots:

- 4 – 2 1/4″ x width of fabric for binding

Solid pink:

- 2 – 2 1/4″ x 5 3/4″ strips
- 2 – 2 1/4″ x 19 1/4″ strips

Black and white stripes:

- 2 – 1 1/2″ x 19 1/4″ strips for top and bottom flanges on embroidered block
- 2 – 1 1/2″ x 9 1/4″ strips for side flanges on embroidered block

Vinyl:

- 4 – 5″ x 22 1/4″ strips

PELICAN

A pelican can hold up to three gallons of water in its bill.

QUAIL

In Colombia and Venezuela, a single hard-boiled quail egg is a common topping on hot dogs and hamburgers.

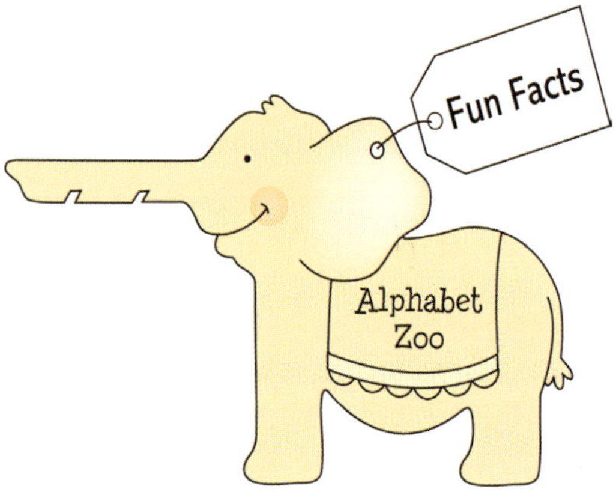

EMBROIDERY

- When preparing your name to embroider, lay it out on the fabric first to make certain that it will fit within a 5 1/4" x 15 1/4" finished block. You may need to reduce or enlarge the name on a photocopier to get a good fit. Refer to the guidelines on page 22-23 for how to color fabric with crayons. Back the crayoned block with muslin. Embroider the block following General Instructions for embroidery on page 10. Trim to 5 3/4" x 15 3/4" making sure the name is centered from side to side and top to bottom.

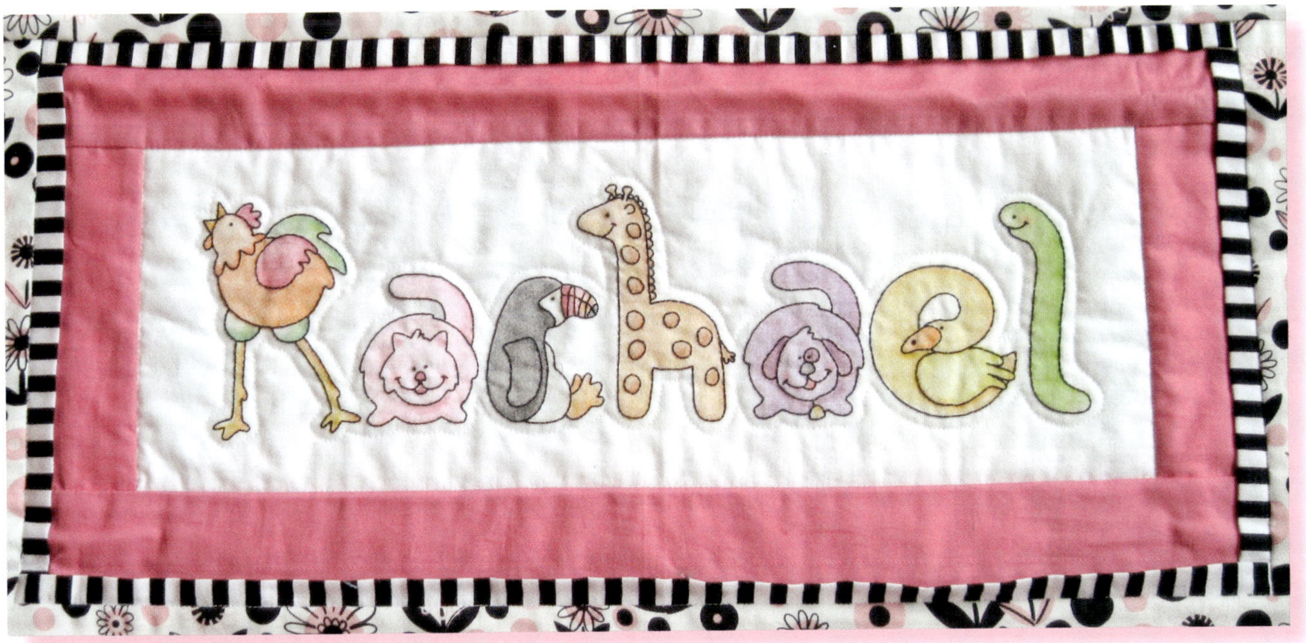

ROOSTER

The rooster is part of the Chinese zodiac. The next "Year of the Rooster" will be 2017. Those born under this sign are believed to be honest, ambitious and quick minded.

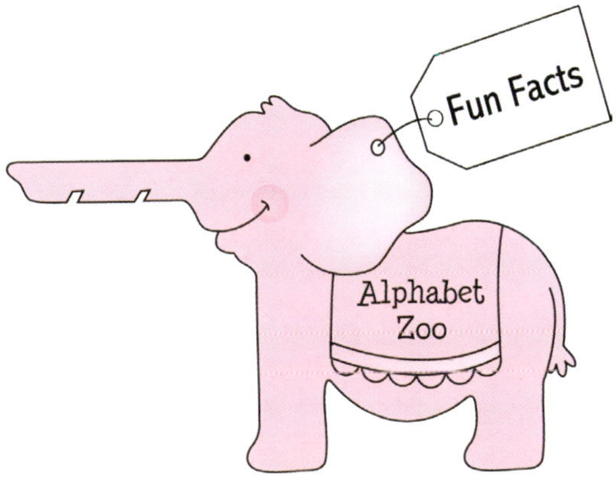

Rachael Hanging Pockets continued

ASSEMBLY

- Stitch pink solid borders to the embroidered block, short sides first, then top and bottom. Press toward the dark fabric.

- Fold strips of black and white striped fabric in half lengthwise to create the flange. Pin short flange sections to the bright flowered side border strips, raw edges together. Stitch. Repeat for the top and bottom of the block.

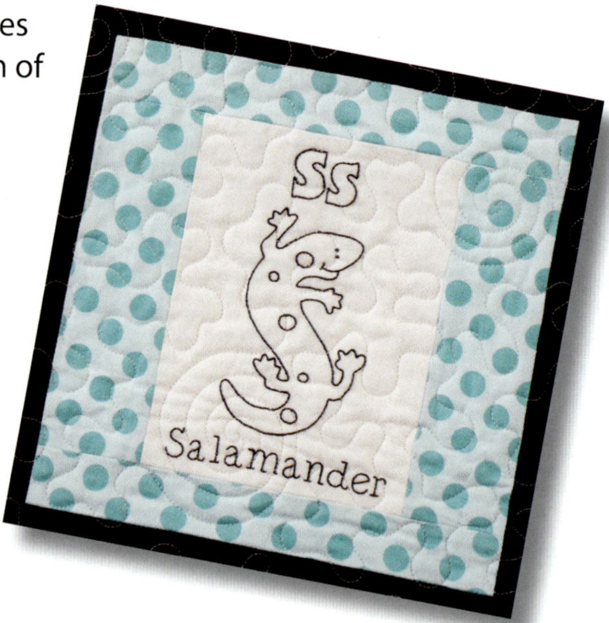

- Add 1 – 2″ x 9 1/4″ flowered strip to each short side of the completed embroidery block.

- Stitch a 4″ x 22 1/4″ strip of flowered fabric along the top of the embroidered block, then stitch a 22 1/4″ x 32 1/2″ piece of flowered fabric to the bottom edge of the block.

- Center and layer the backing, batting and wall hanging top. Pin or hand-baste.

- If you wish to have overall quilting, do this now. You will not be able to quilt the lower portion of the wall hanging after the vinyl has been added.

- Square and trim.

SALAMANDER

Some salamanders have tongues that measure 10 times the length of their bodies.

TIGER

There are more tigers kept as pets than there are tigers in the wild. Most tigers have more than 100 stripes.

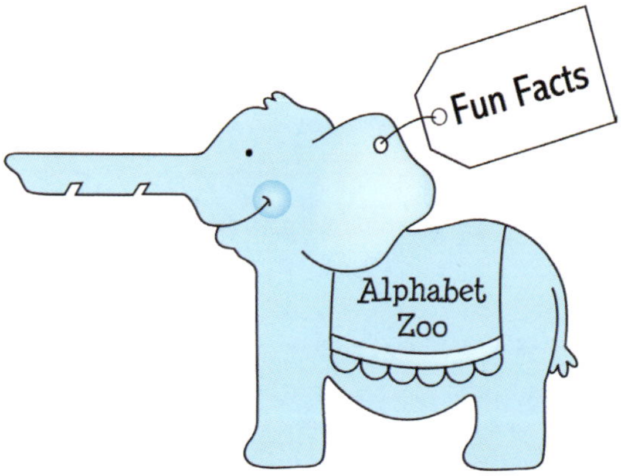

VINYL POCKETS

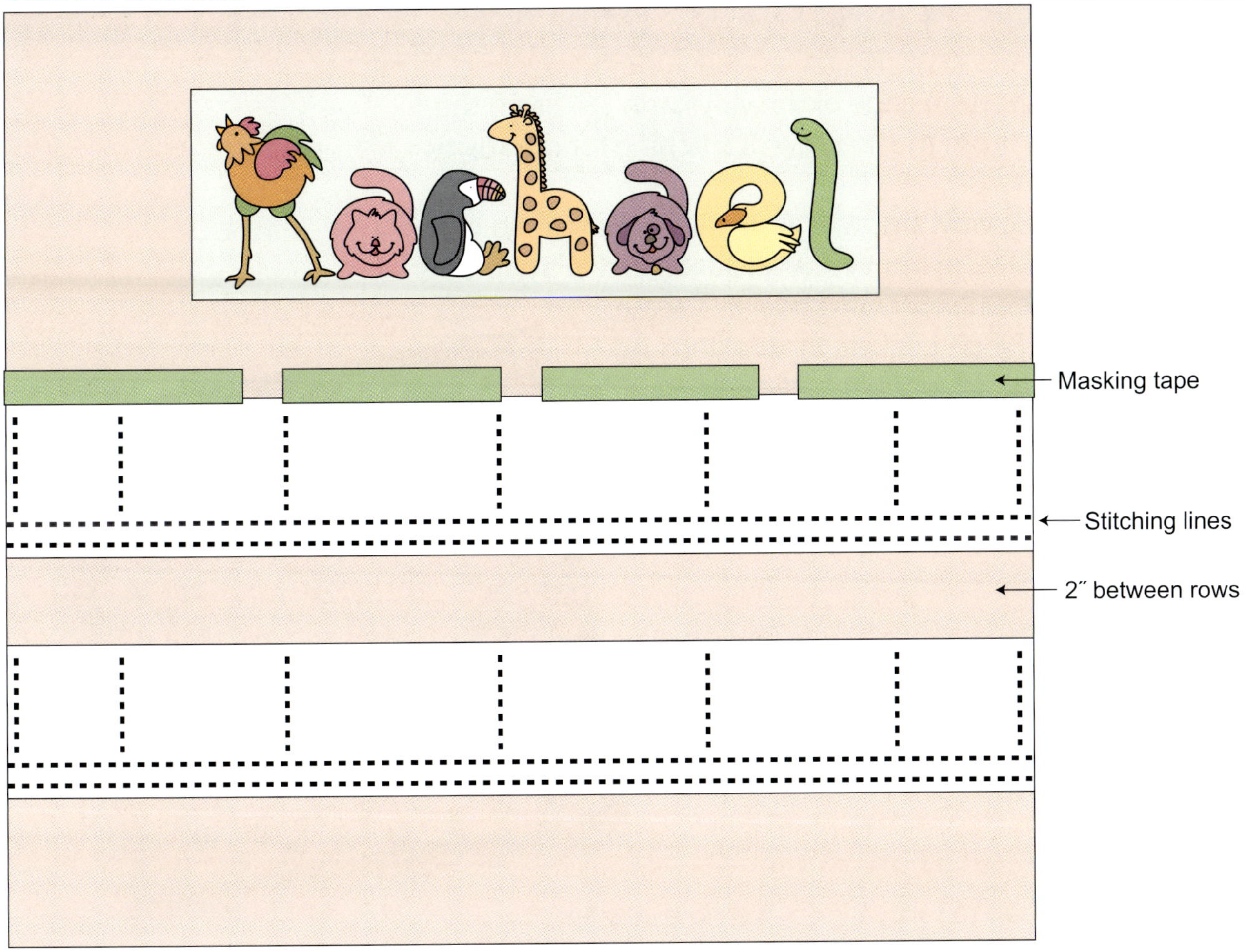

- Refer to the pocket guide for making the vinyl pockets.

- Measure 2″ down from the seam at the bottom of the embroidered block and draw a line across the width. Place the top edge of a vinyl strip along this line and baste it to the fabric with masking tape. Do not use pins, as they will leave permanent holes in the vinyl.

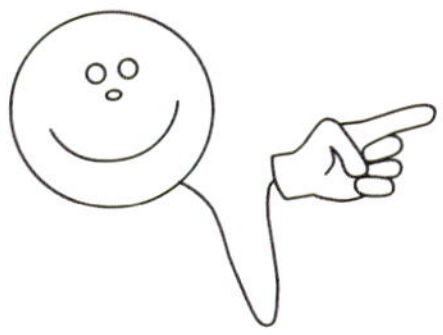

TIP: *Stick a little bit of masking tape to the underside of your presser foot for good traction.*

Rachael Hanging Pockets continued

- Stitch across the bottom edge of the vinyl strip 1/4" from the edge. Repeat 1/8" from the first row of stitching for durability.

- Machine-baste the vinyl strip 1/8" from each side to hold it in place. Measure 1 1/4" in from each side and stitch a double vertical line to create a narrow vinyl pocket. Create three more 6 1/2" wide pockets by marking and stitching the vinyl with double vertical lines.

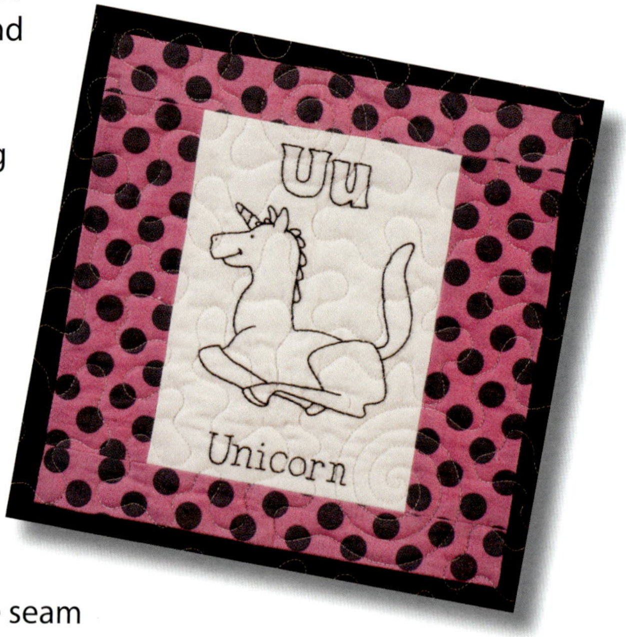

- Repeat for the remaining 3 vinyl strips, placing each one 2" below the one above it.

HANGING TABS

- Make 3 hanging tabs. For each tab, fold a 4 1/2" x 5 1/2" flowered strip in half lengthwise, right sides together. Stitch a 1/4" seam along the long edge, creating a tube. Turn right side out. Press seam to the center of the back of the tube.

- Fold the tube in half to form a loop, hiding the seam inside the loop. Center one tab on the back of the wall hanging along the top edge, raw edges together. Baste. Repeat for the remaining 2 tabs, attaching them about 2" in from the outside borders.

FINISHING

- Bind hanging pocket, making certain tabs are sewn into the binding. After binding, bring each tab up, press and hand stitch in place to the backside of the binding.

UNICORN

According to medieval mythology, a cup made of spiraled unicorn horn would protect against any poisons that might be added to its contents.

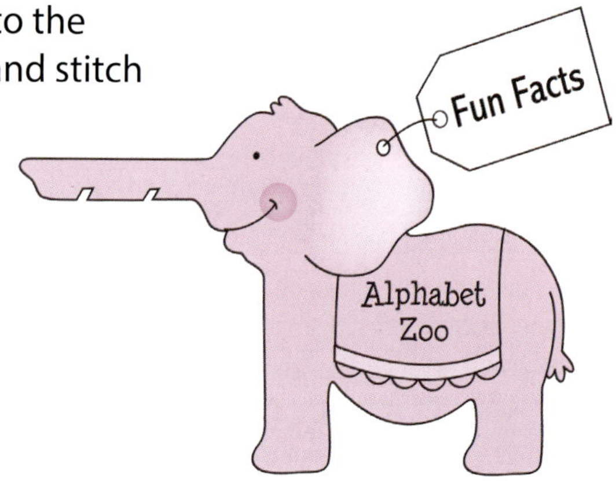

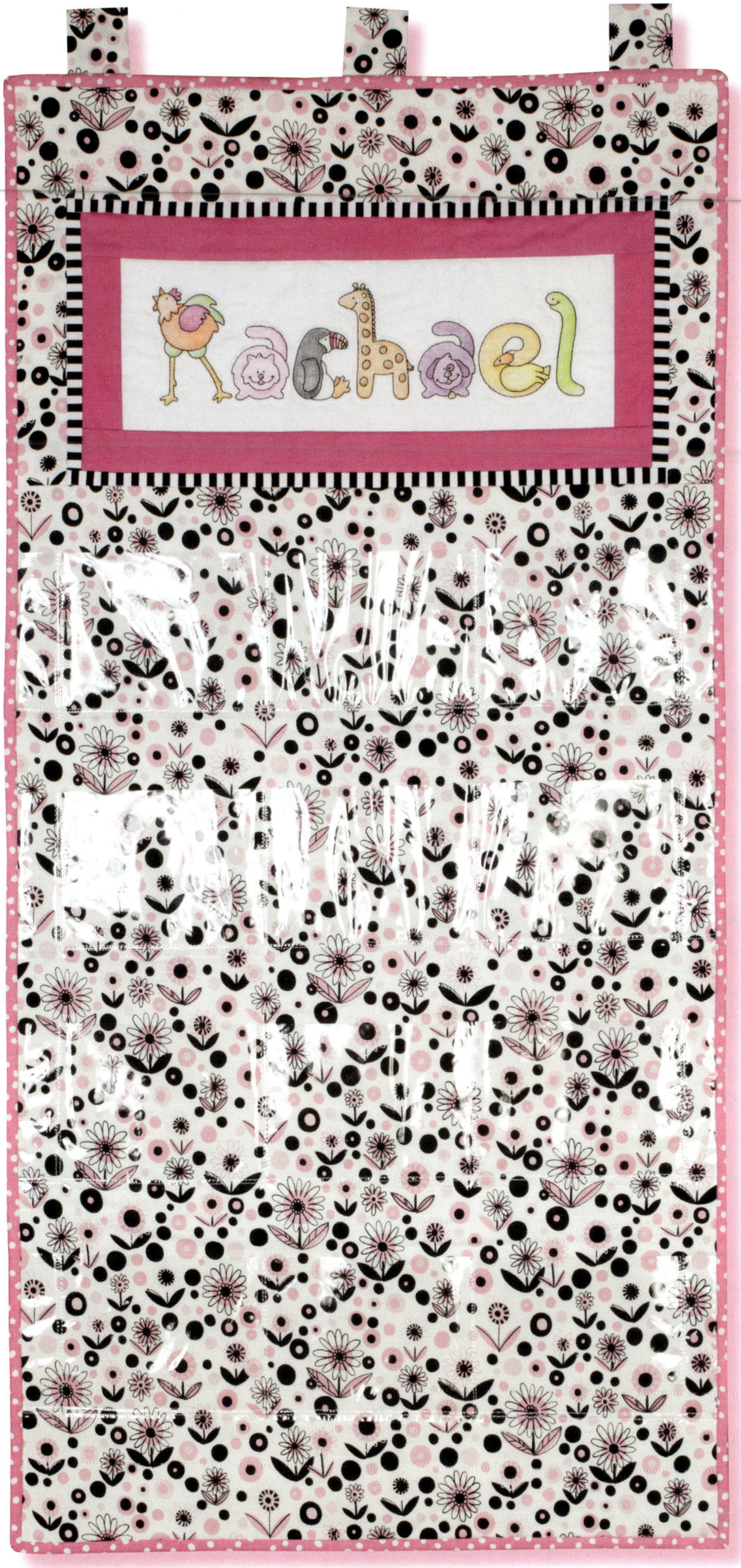
Rachael

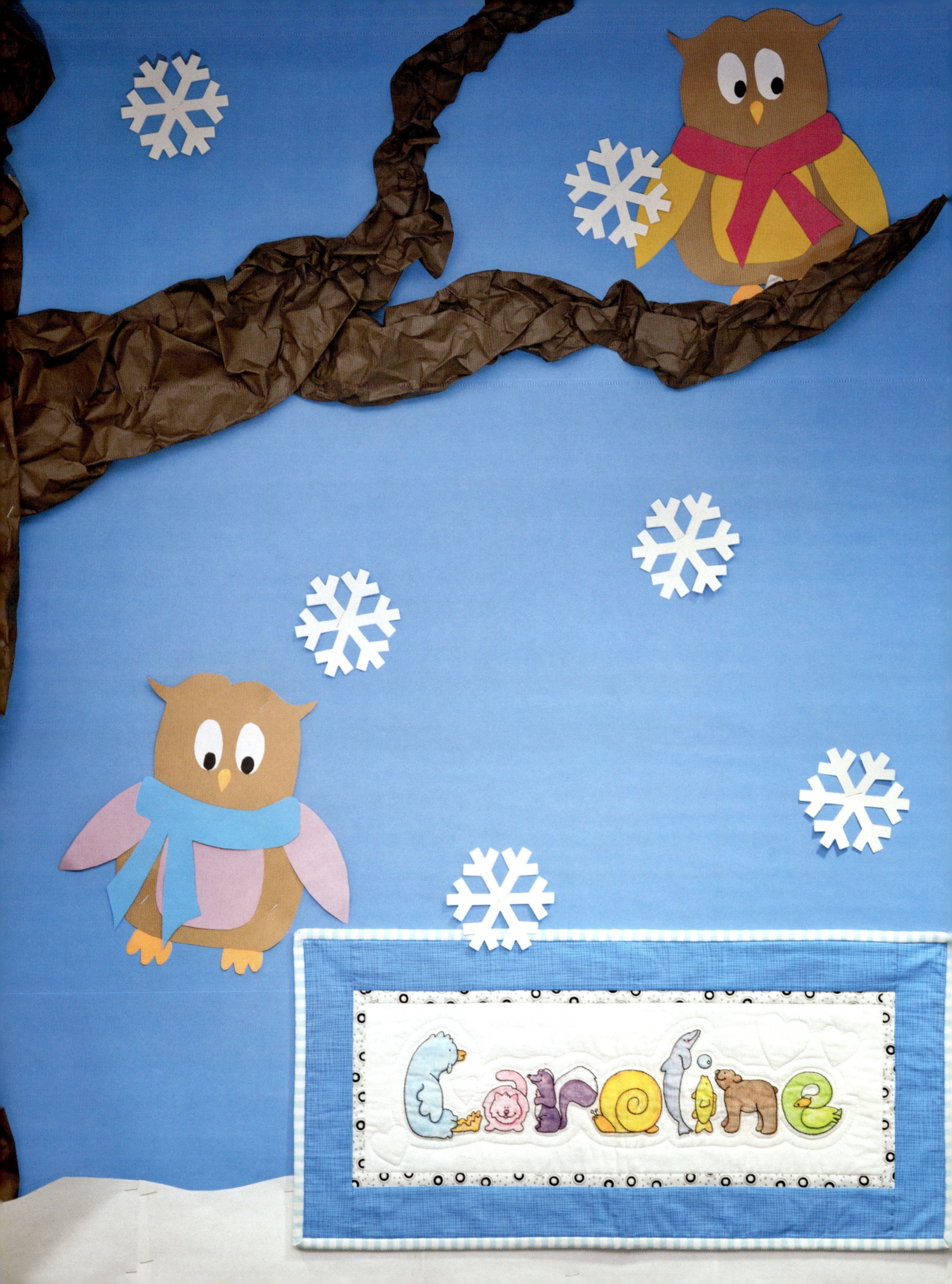
Caroline

Caroline

This colorful banner has your name written all over it!

These Alphabet Zoo names began many years ago as hand-drawn artwork done with a pen and colored pencils on plain paper. I love the evolution to fabric, crayons and embroidery floss.

FABRIC AND SUPPLIES

Yardage listed is sufficient for an average length name, such as Caroline.

- White solid: 1/2 yard
- Muslin: 1/2 yard for backing embroidery
- White with black dot print: 1/8 yard
- Medium blue: 1/4 yard
- Blue and white stripe: 1/8 yard for binding
- Batting (90″ wide): 1/3 yard
- Backing: 1/2 yard
- Embroidery floss: DMC Perle Cotton size 12 in #310 Black
- Embroidery needle
- Crayola crayons

Finished banner measures 10 1/4″ high; length is determined by length of name

CUTTING INSTRUCTIONS

White solid *and* Muslin:

- 1 large rectangle each, about 12″ high x the length of the name plus 6″ (LON)

White with black dot print:

- 2 – 1″ x 7 1/2″ strips for flange
- 2 strips – 1″ x LON for the flange

Medium blue:

- 2 – 2 1/4″ x 11 1/4″ strips for border
- 2 – 2 1/4″ x LON strips for border

Blue and white stripe:

- 2 – 2 1/4″ x width of fabric (WOF) strips for binding

Caroline continued

ASSEMBLY

- Refer to Coloring on Fabric on page 8, and use Crayola crayons to color the design. Back the crayoned block with the muslin. Embroider the block following the General Instructions for Embroidery on page 10. Carefully center the name and trim the block to 6 3/4" high. Measure about 1 1/2" from either end of the name and trim.

- Fold the polka-dot fabric strips in half lengthwise to create the flange. Matching raw edges, with right sides together, stitch the flange to the top and bottom of the embroidered block and then to the sides.

- Sew the medium blue borders to the top and bottom, and then to the sides. Press.

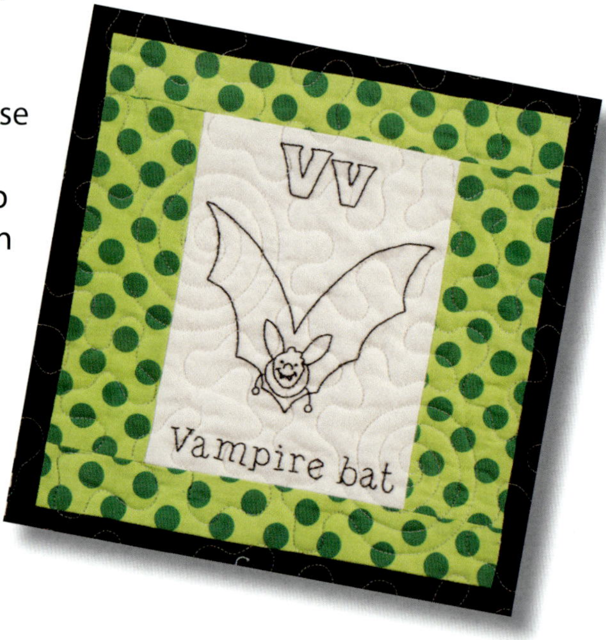

FINISHING

- Quilt as desired, square, trim and bind.

VAMPIRE BAT

Bats are the only mammal with the ability to fly. They are the only species of bat that can also walk, jump and run.

WORM

Depending on the soil quality, there can be anywhere from 250,000 to 1.75 million earthworms per acre of land.

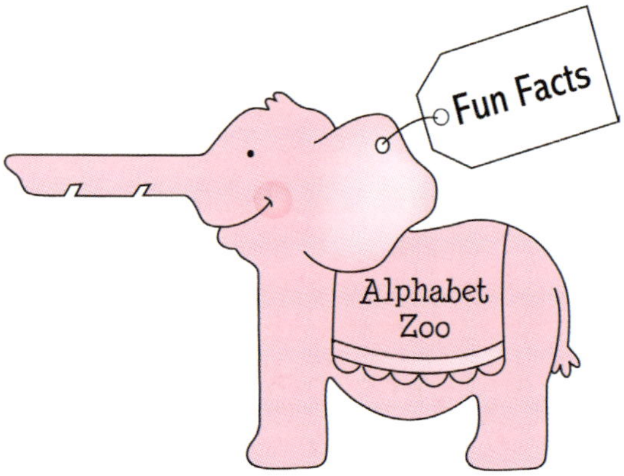

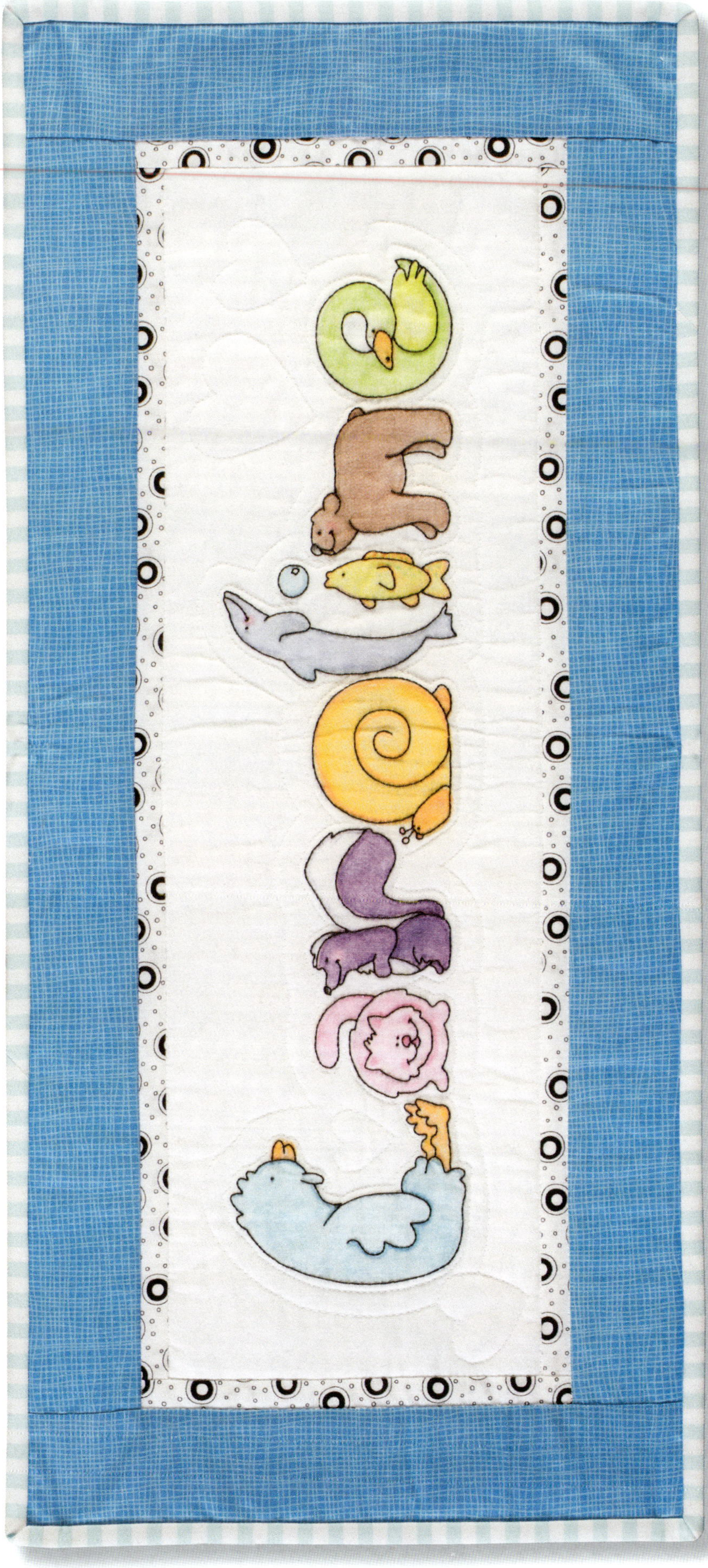

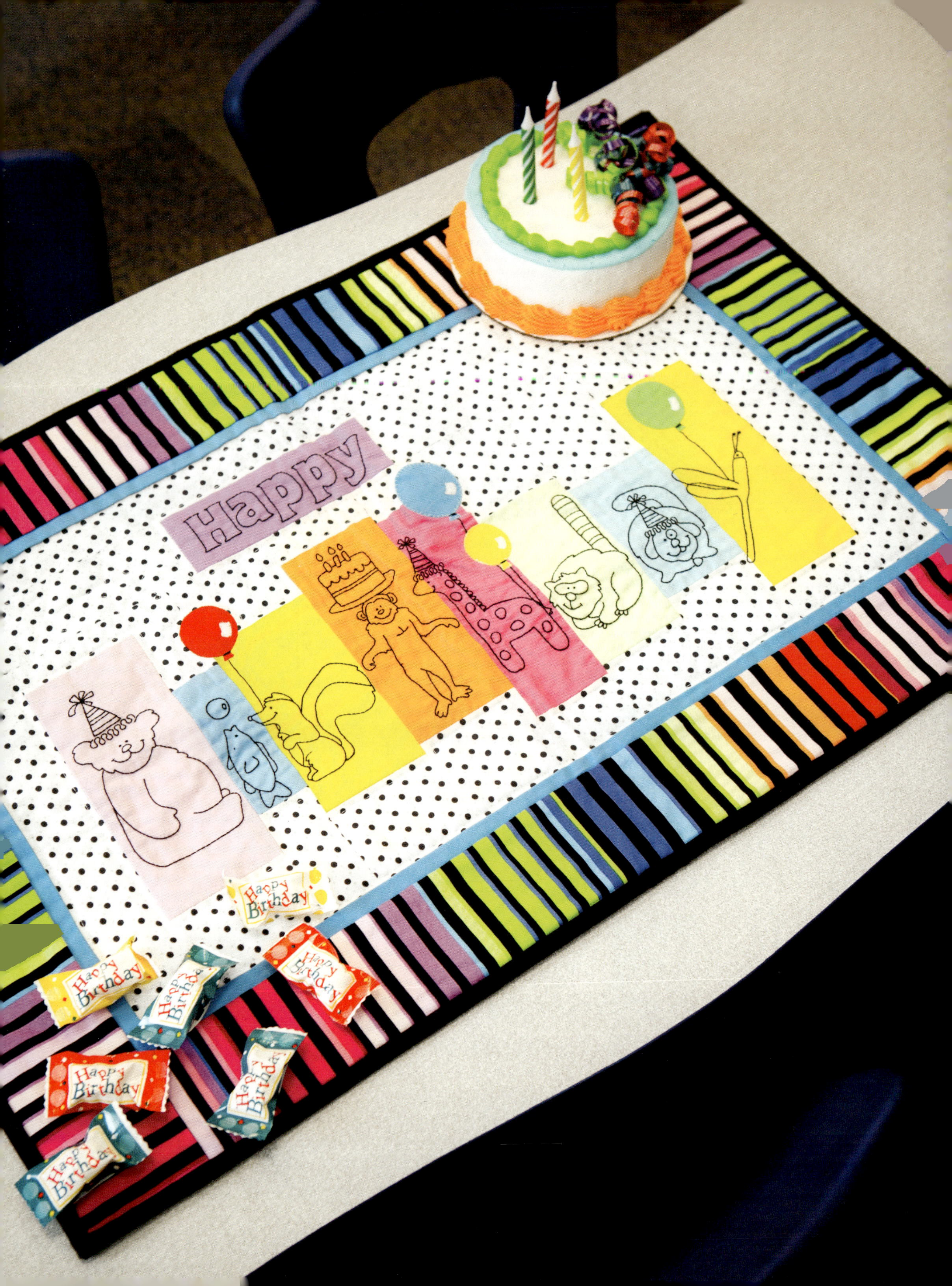
HAPPY
Happy Birthday

Happy Birthday

A birthday celebration isn't complete without party hats, cake and balloons!

When my kids were little, I made birthday banners for them from butcher paper and letters cut from colored construction paper or giftwrap. This joyful quilted birthday banner will last from one birthday to another, throughout the years. It's the perfect size to hang on a door or above a child's bed on that special day.

Finished banner measures 18" x 27"
Embroidery design and template on pages 76 & 77.

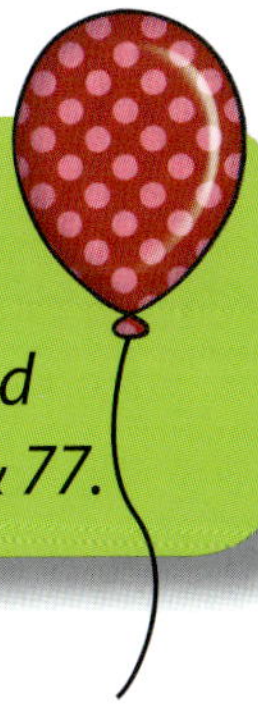

FABRIC AND SUPPLIES

- White with black polka dots: 1/3 yard
- Multi-color stripes: 1/4 yard
- Medium blue solid: 1/4 yard
- Yellow solid: 8" x 10" scrap
- Small scraps approximately 4" x 8" each of solids in light purple, orange, pink, pale green, medium purple, light blue, green and red, or any colors that you want
- White muslin: 1/2 yard for backing embroidery
- Solid black for binding: 1/4 yard
- Batting (90" wide): 3/4 yard
- Backing: 2/3 yard
- Fusible web
- Embroidery floss: DMC Perle Cotton size 12 in #310 Black
- 5" or 7" embroidery hoop
- Embroidery needle size 8
- Pigma pen or Frixion pen

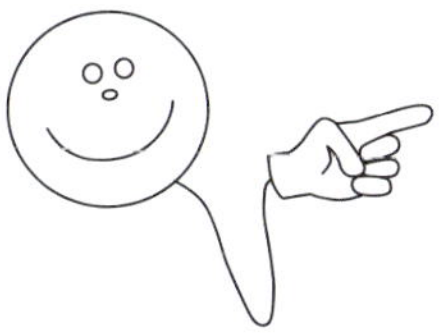

TIP: *When using colored fabrics on an embroidery project like this one, the task of tracing your design will be made much easier if you choose lightweight fabrics.*

Happy Birthday continued

CUTTING INSTRUCTIONS

White with black polka dots:
- 2 – 1 3/4″ x 3 1/2″ strips
- 6 – 3″ x 3 1/2″ strips
- 4 – 2 3/4″ x 3 1/2″ strips
- 2 – 2 1/2″ x 3 1/2″ strips
- 2 – 3 1/4″ x 3 1/2″ strips
- 2 – 2 1/2″ x 9 3/4″ strips
- 1 – 2 1/2″ x 9 3/4″ strip
- 1 – 2 1/2″ x 7 1/4″ strip
- 1 – 2″ x 22″ strip

Multi-color stripes:
- 2 – 3″ x 22″ for top and bottom borders
- 2 – 3″ x 18 1/4″ for side borders

Medium blue solid:
- 1 – 1 3/4″ x 4 1/4″ rectangle
- 2 – 1 1/4″ x 12 3/4″ for flange
- 2 – 1 1/4″ x 13 1/4″ for flange
- One large balloon

Yellow solid:
- 1 – 3″ x 5 1/2″ rectangle
- 1 – 3″ x 7″ rectangle
- 1 small balloon

Light purple solid:
- 1 – 3 1/4″ x 7″ rectangle

Orange solid:
- 1 – 3″ x 6 1/4″ rectangle

Pink solid:
- 1 – 2 1/2″ x 6 3/4″ rectangle

Pale green solid:
- 1 – 2 3/4″ x 5 1/4″ rectangle

Light blue solid:
- 1 – 2 3/4″ x 3 3/4″ rectangle

Medium purple solid:
- 1 – 2 1/2″ x 6″ rectangle

Green solid:
- 1 medium balloon

Red solid:
- 1 medium balloon

White muslin:
- 1 – 15″ x 25″ piece to back embroidery

Black solid:
- 3 – 2 1/4″ x width of fabric

XYSTICUS ULMI

This slow-moving spider does not build a web, but rather ambushes its prey.

YABBY

These freshwater crustaceans, native to Australia, scavenge for their food. They are similar to, but generally smaller than, lobsters.

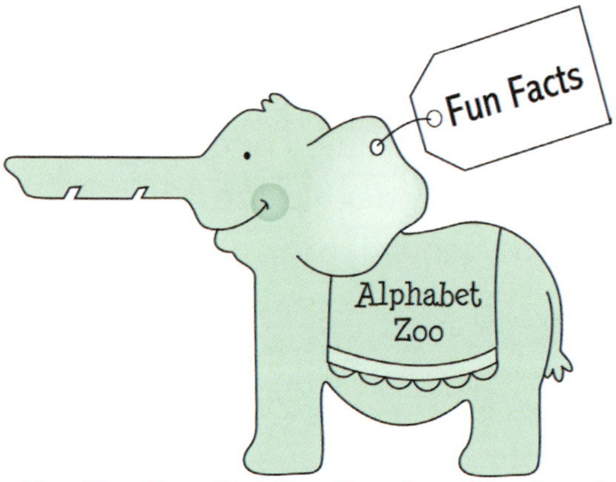

ASSEMBLY

- Using the assembly guide as an example, and matching widths, stitch a polka-dot strip to each narrow end of a light purple, medium blue, yellow, orange, pink, pale green and light blue solid rectangle.

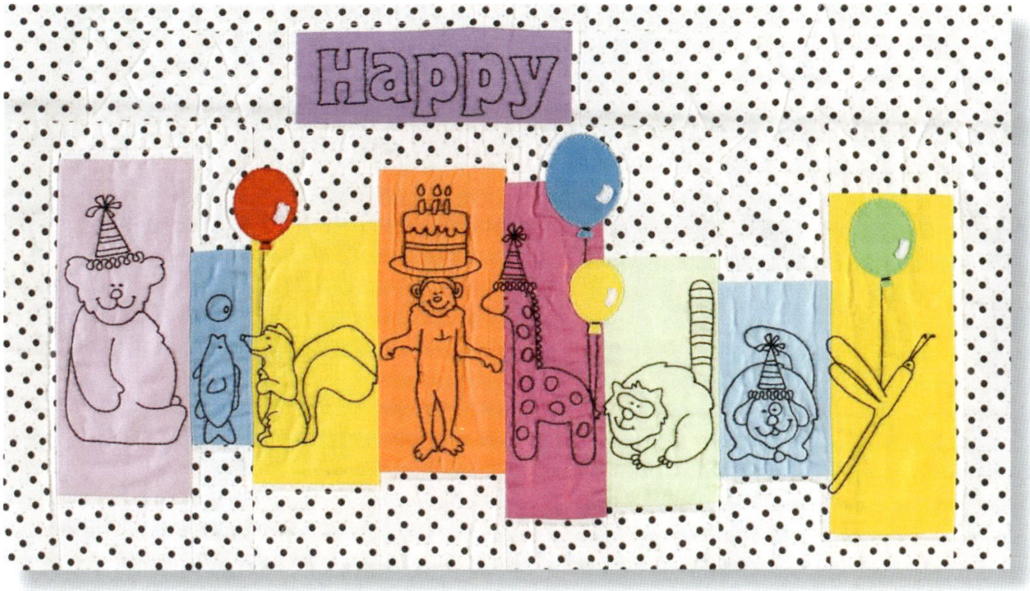

- Arrange and stitch the pieced strips vertically, in the order listed above, so that the solid colors are staggered. End with a second yellow pieced strip. The result will be a block with uneven borders. Trim the block to measure 9 3/4" high x 18" wide.

HAPPY BIRTHDAY ASSEMBLY GUIDE

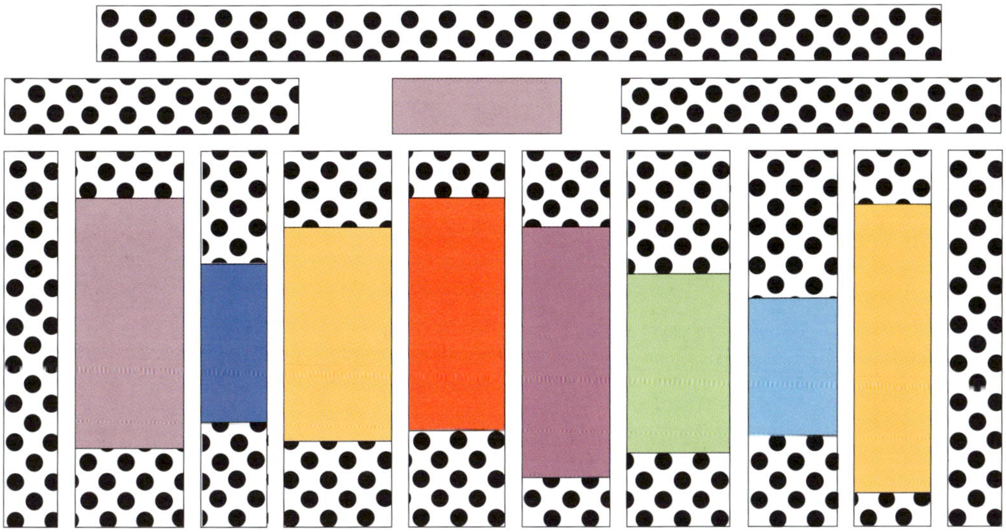

Happy Birthday continued

- Add a 2 1/2" x 9 3/4" polka-dot strip to each side of trimmed block. Add a 2 1/2" x 9 3/4" polka-dot strip to each to each side of trimmed block.

- Stitch a 2 1/2" x 7 1/4" polka-dot strip to a narrow end of the dark purple rectangle. Stitch a 2 1/2" x 9 3/4" polka-dot strip to the other end. Sew this pieced strip to the upper edge of the trimmed block with the shorter polka-dot piece to the left.

- Add a 2" x 22" polka-dot strip to the top edge.

- Trace "Birthday" animals from the template on page 76 and 77 onto the colored rectangles. Some of the animals will share portions of two color blocks.

- Trace "Happy" letters onto the dark purple rectangle at the top.

- Back the entire block with muslin and embroider following the General Instructions on page 9-11.

- Apply fusible webbing to the reverse side of the small scraps of red, green, pink and yellow solids. Cut balloons from these scraps using the template on page 76 and 77.

- Using the photograph as a guide, fuse the balloons to the banner and blanket stitch the edges, or use your favorite appliqué method.

- Add a spot of "shine" to the balloons with a dab of white fabric paint or a few satin stitches of white embroidery floss.

- Fold strips of medium solid blue fabric in half lengthwise to create the flange. Stitch the short flange sections to the sides of the embroidered block, raw edges together. Repeat for the top and bottom.

- Add a 3" x 22" multi-colored stripe strip to the top and bottom of the block, then stitch a 3" x 18 1/4" striped fabric strip to a side for the borders.

FINISHING

Quilt as desired and bind.

ZORILLA

The zorilla is considered by those in-the-know (or is that "in the nose?") to be THE smelliest animal on Earth.

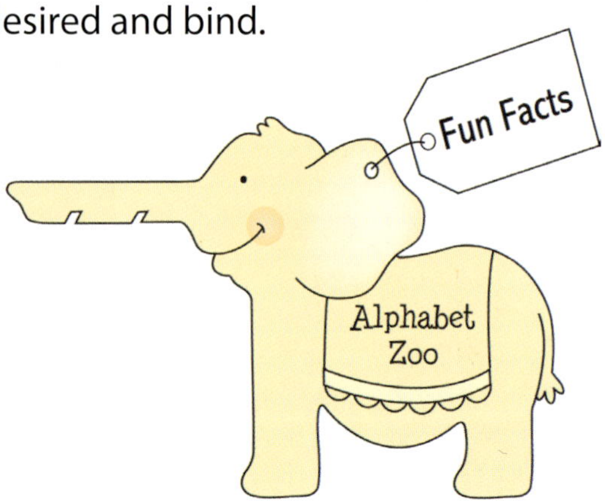

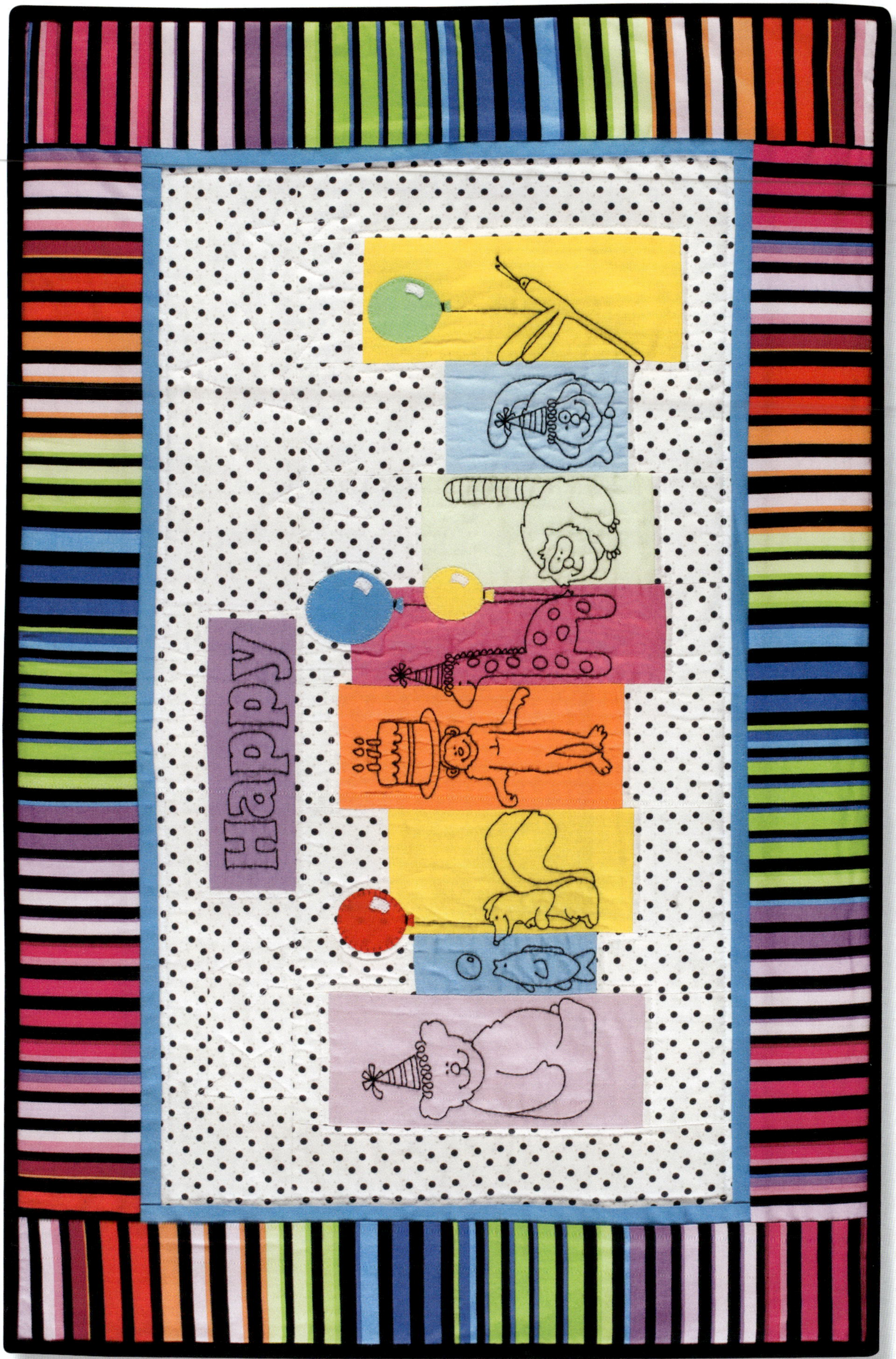
Happy

Templates

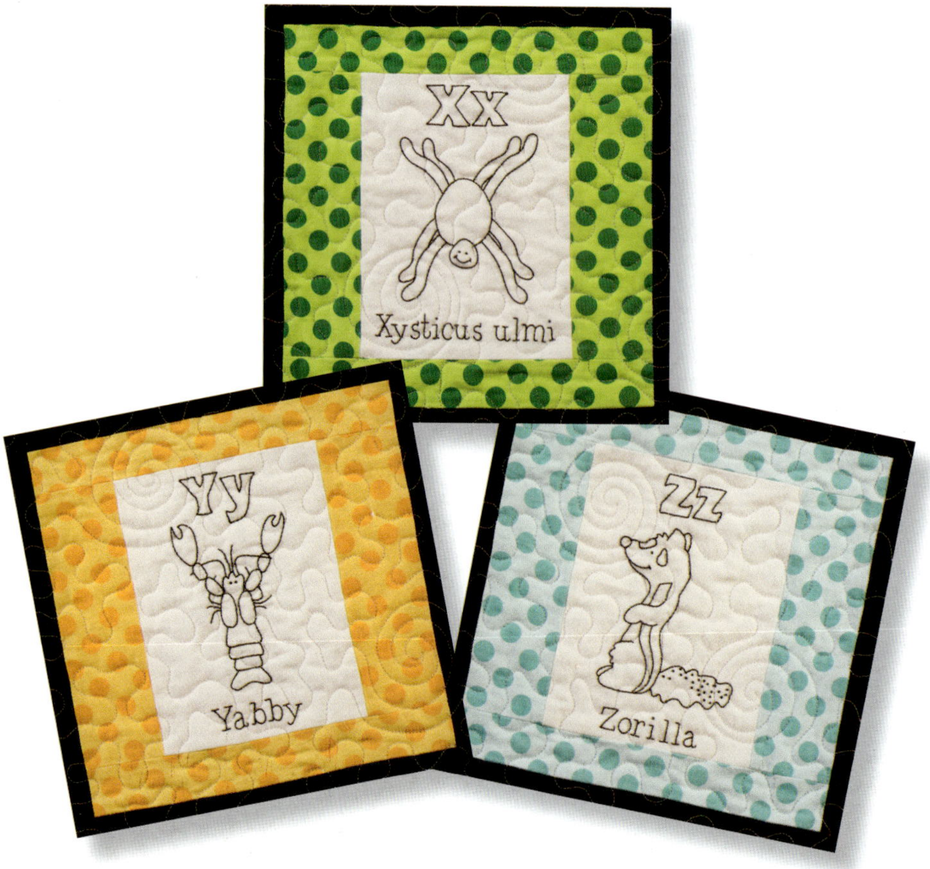

Aa

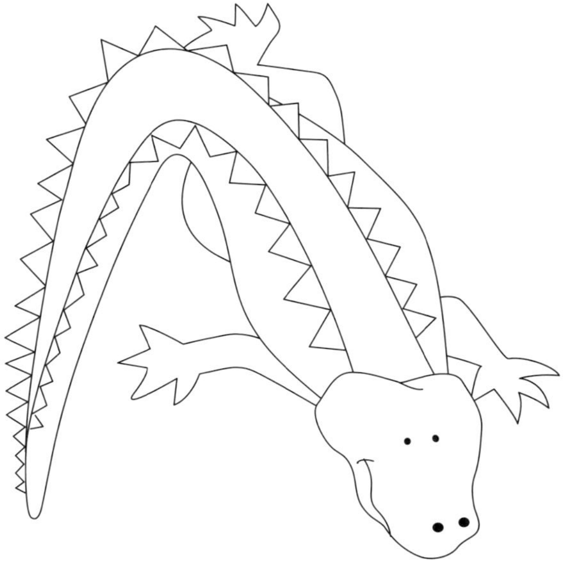

Alligator

Bb

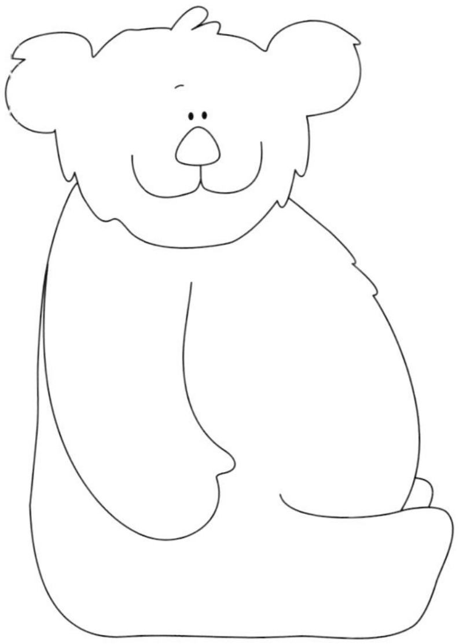

Bear

Cc

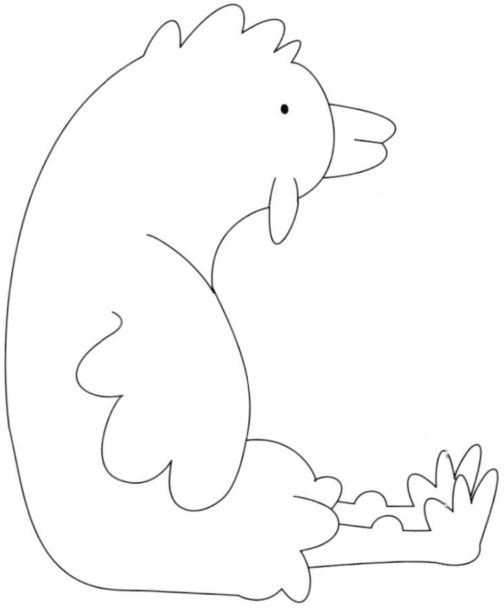

Chicken

Dd

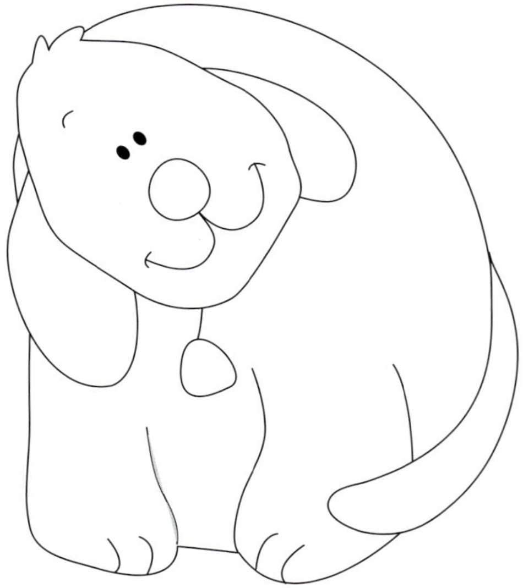

Dog

Ee

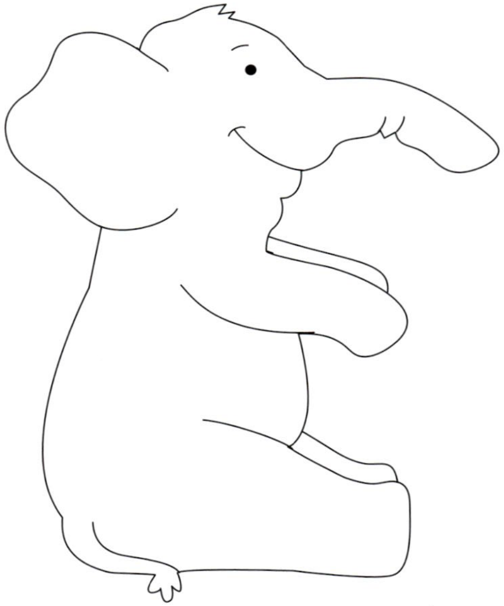

Elephant

Ff

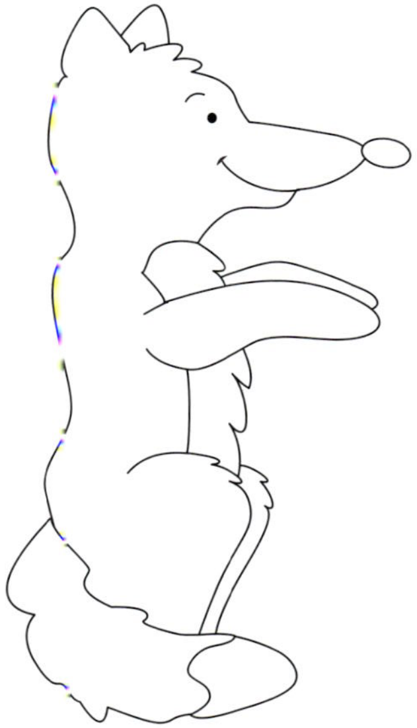

Fox

Gg Hh Ii Jj

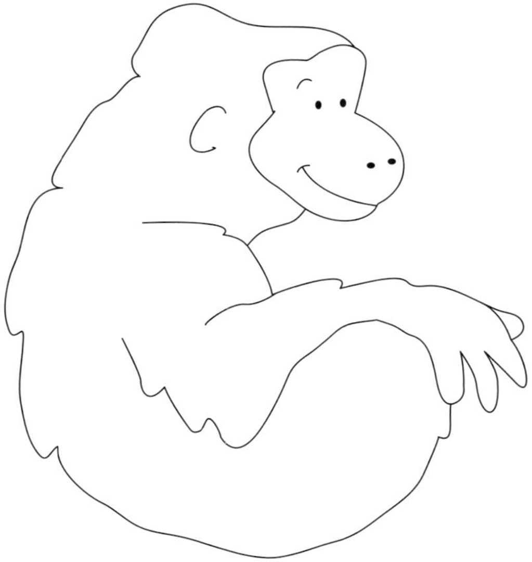
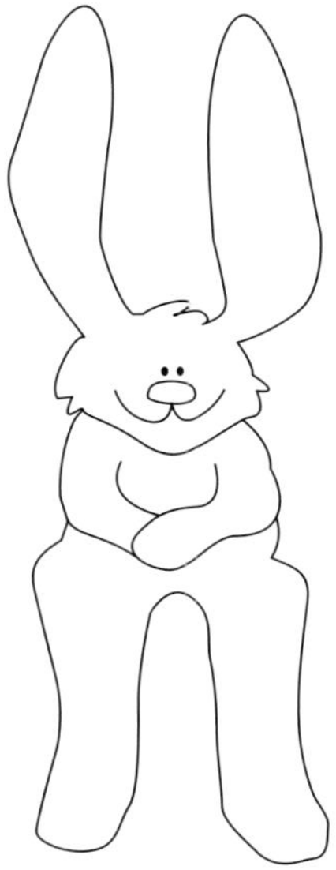
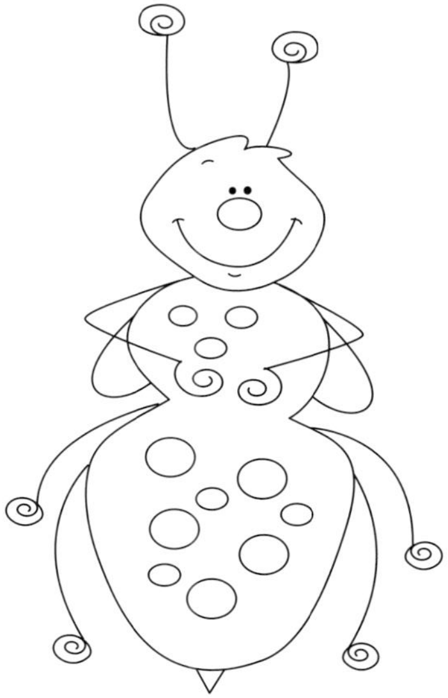
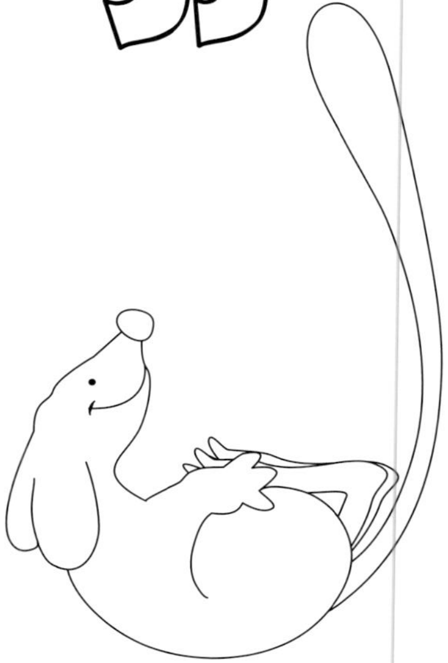

Gorilla Hare Insect Jerboa

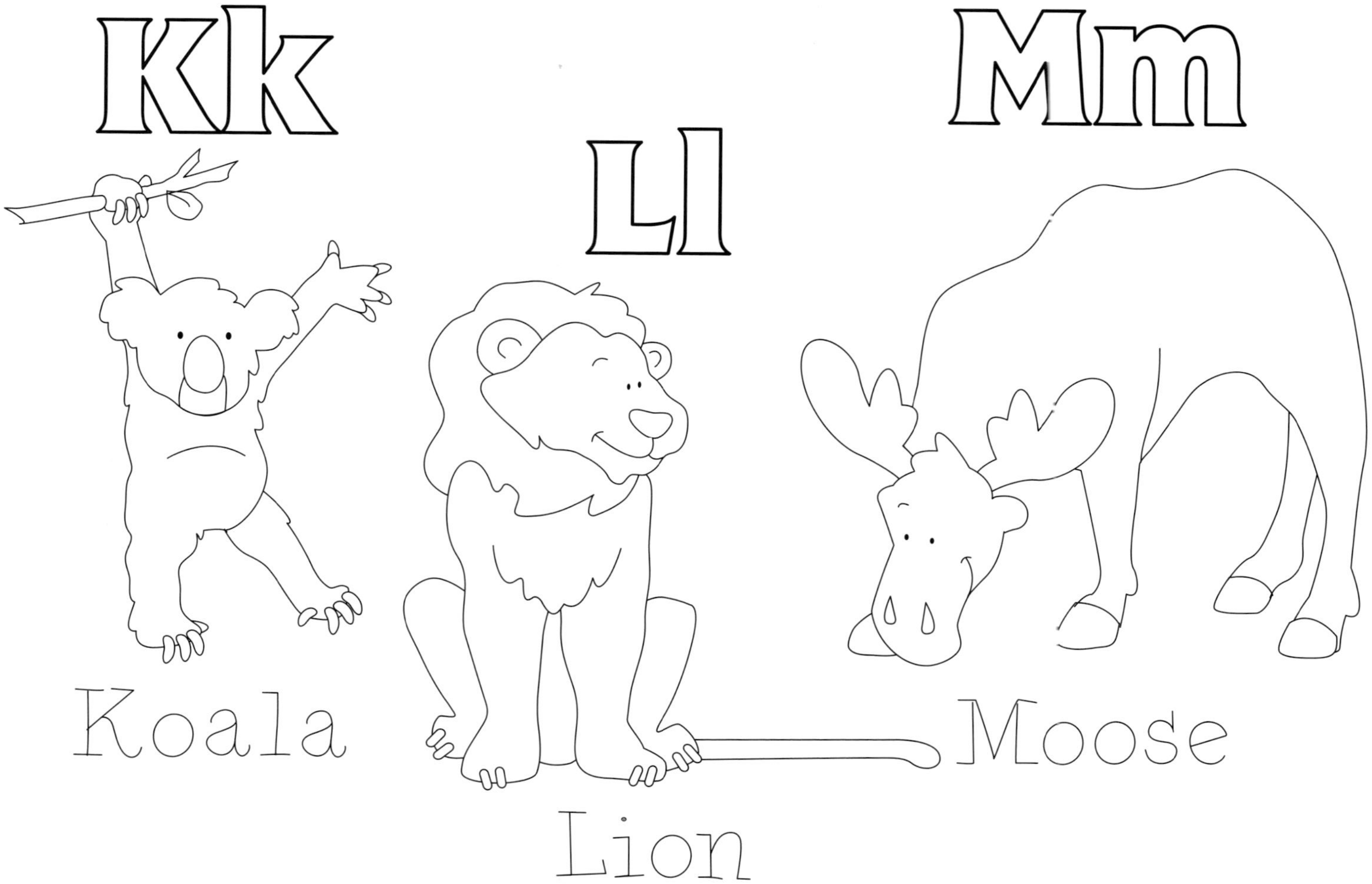
Kk
Ll
Mm
Koala
Lion
Moose

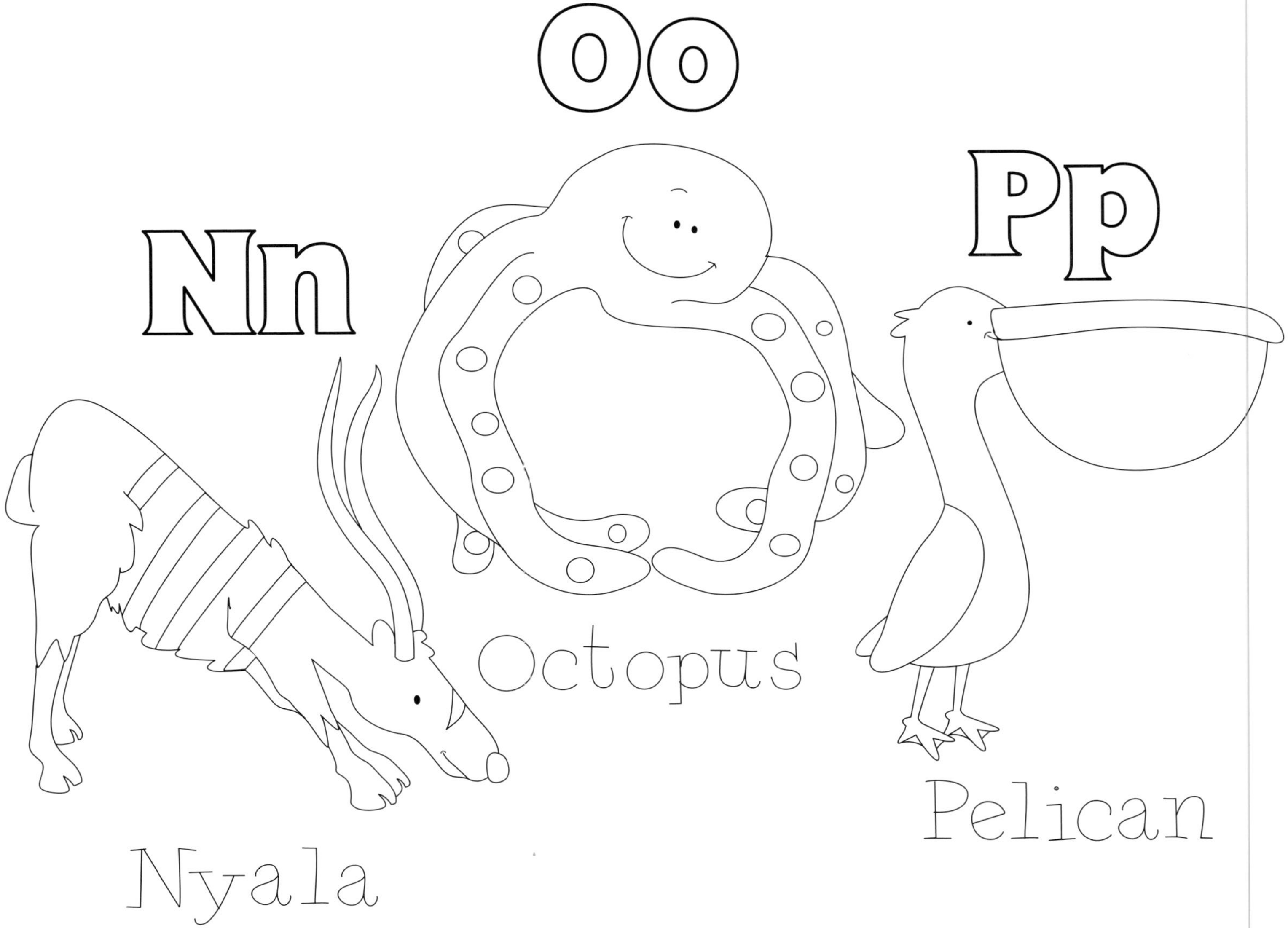
Nn
Oo
Pp
Nyala
Octopus
Pelican

Qq

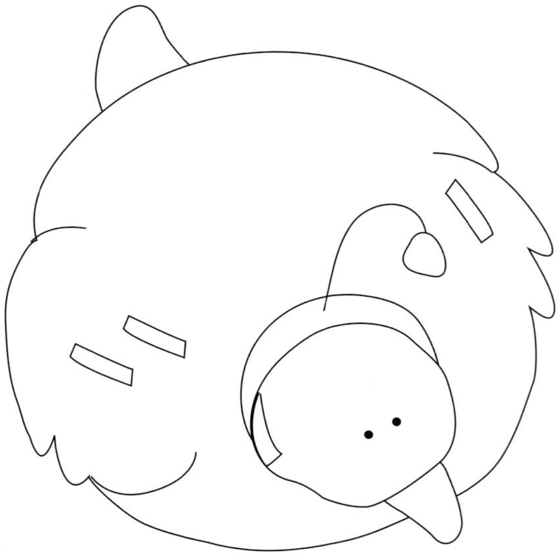

Quail

Rr

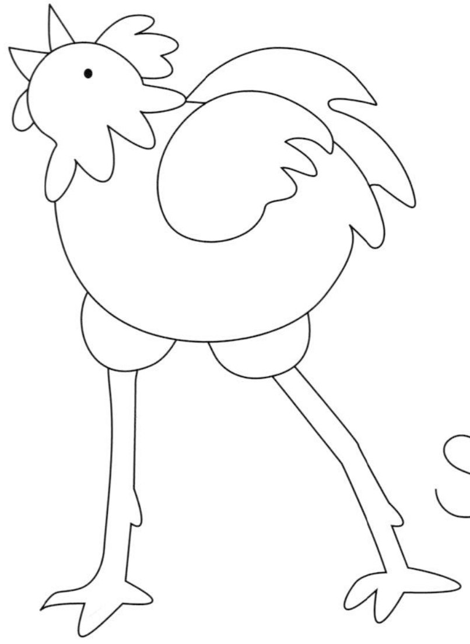

Rooster

Ss

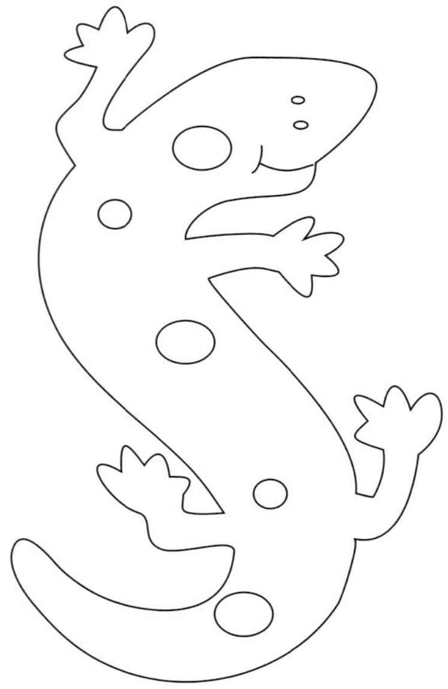

Salamander

Tt

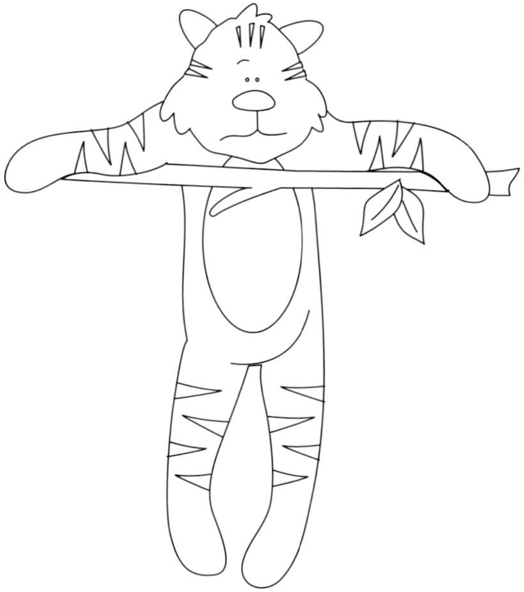

Tiger

Uu

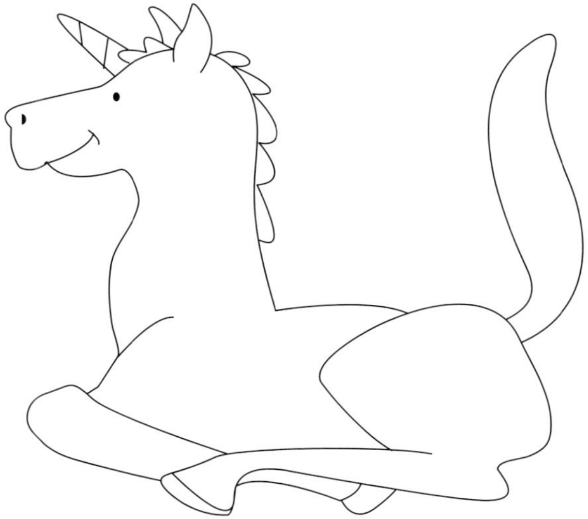

Unicorn

Vv

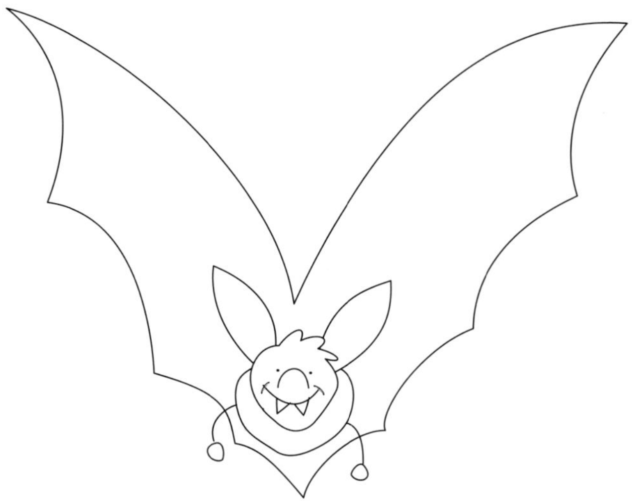

Vampire bat

Ww

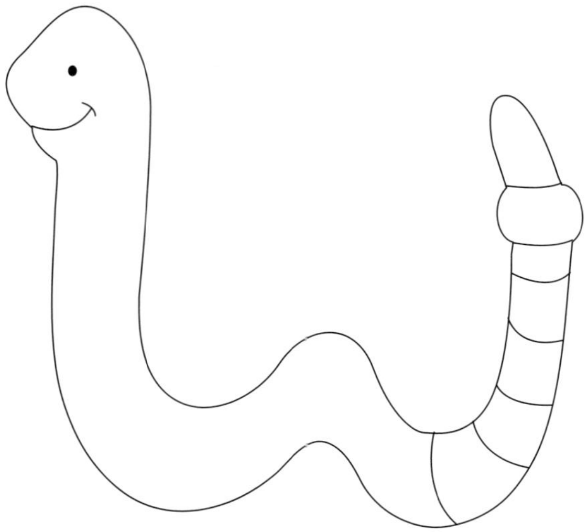

Worm

Xx

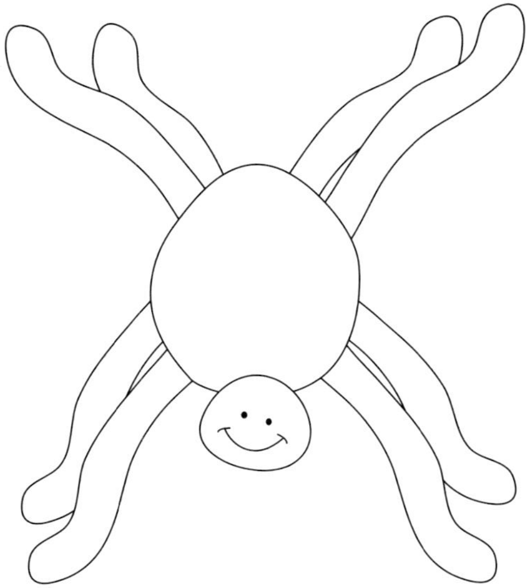

Xysticus ulmi

Yy

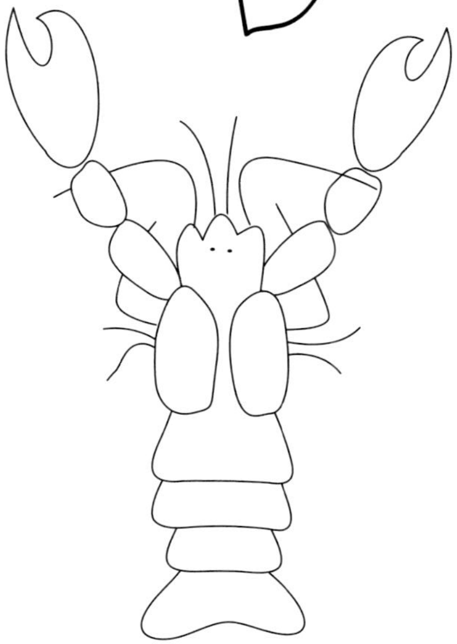

Yabby

Zz

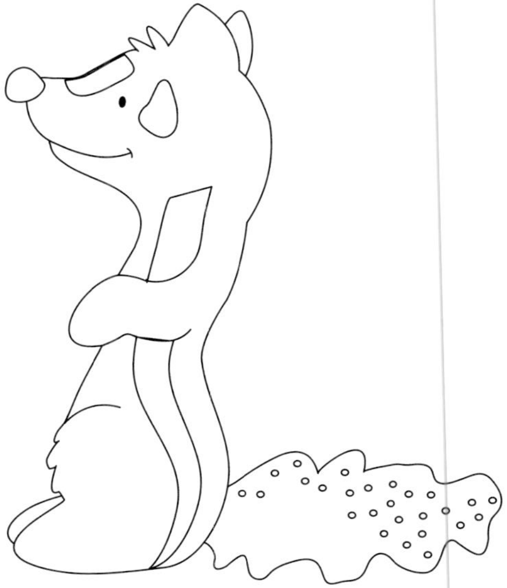

Zorilla

An animal can be transformed into several different letters with a new tail.

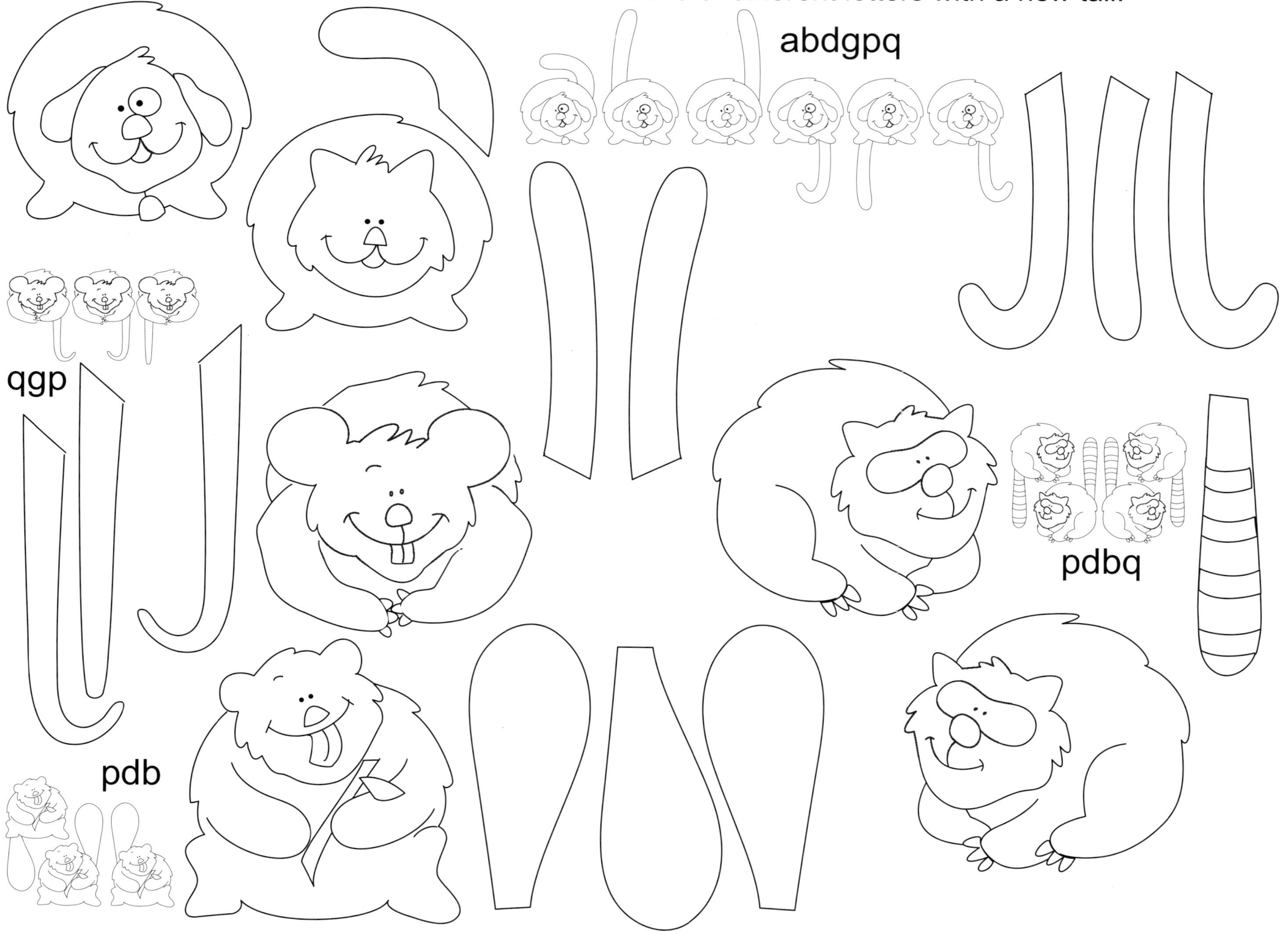

An animal can be transformed into several different letters with a new tail.

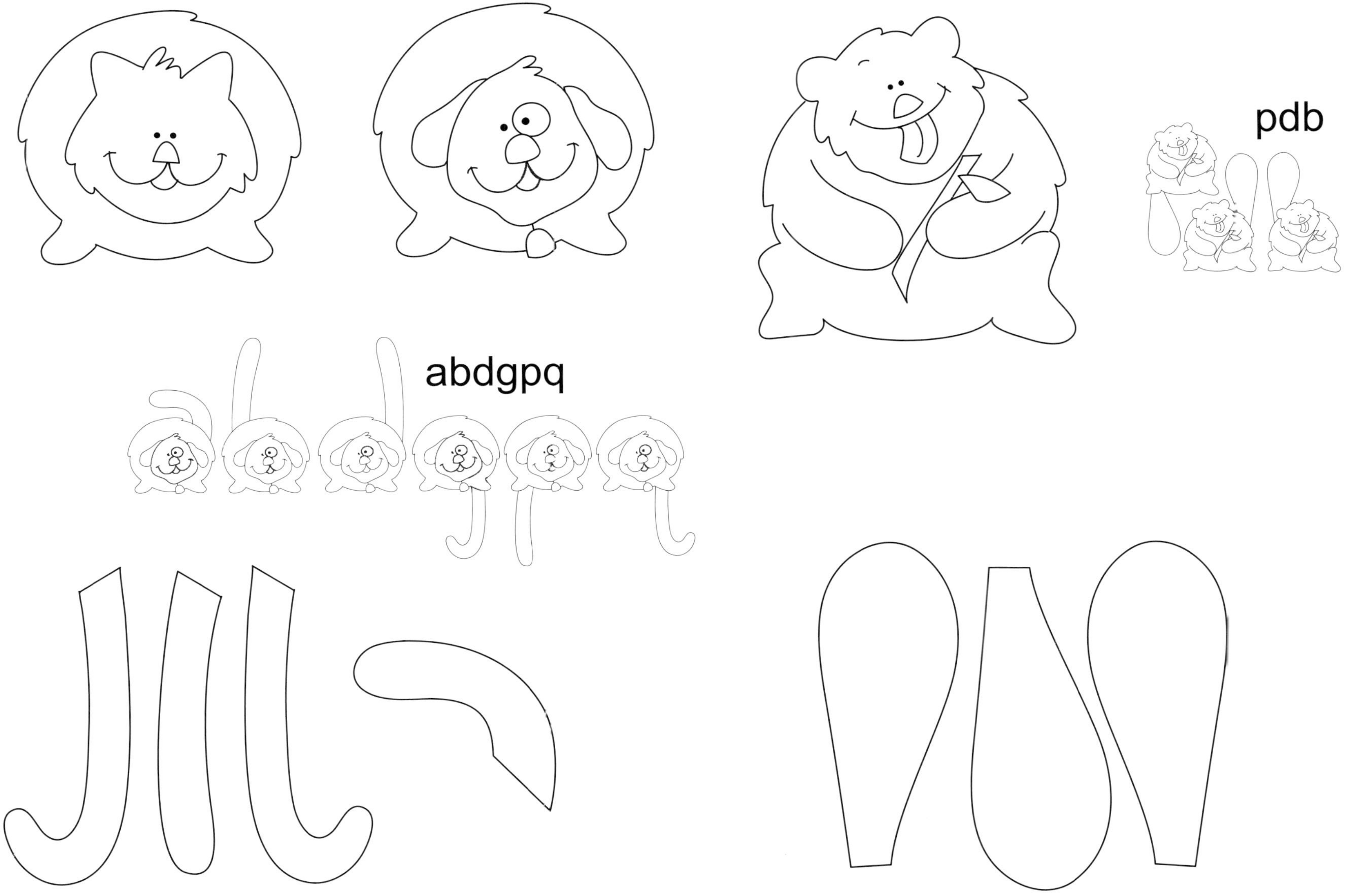

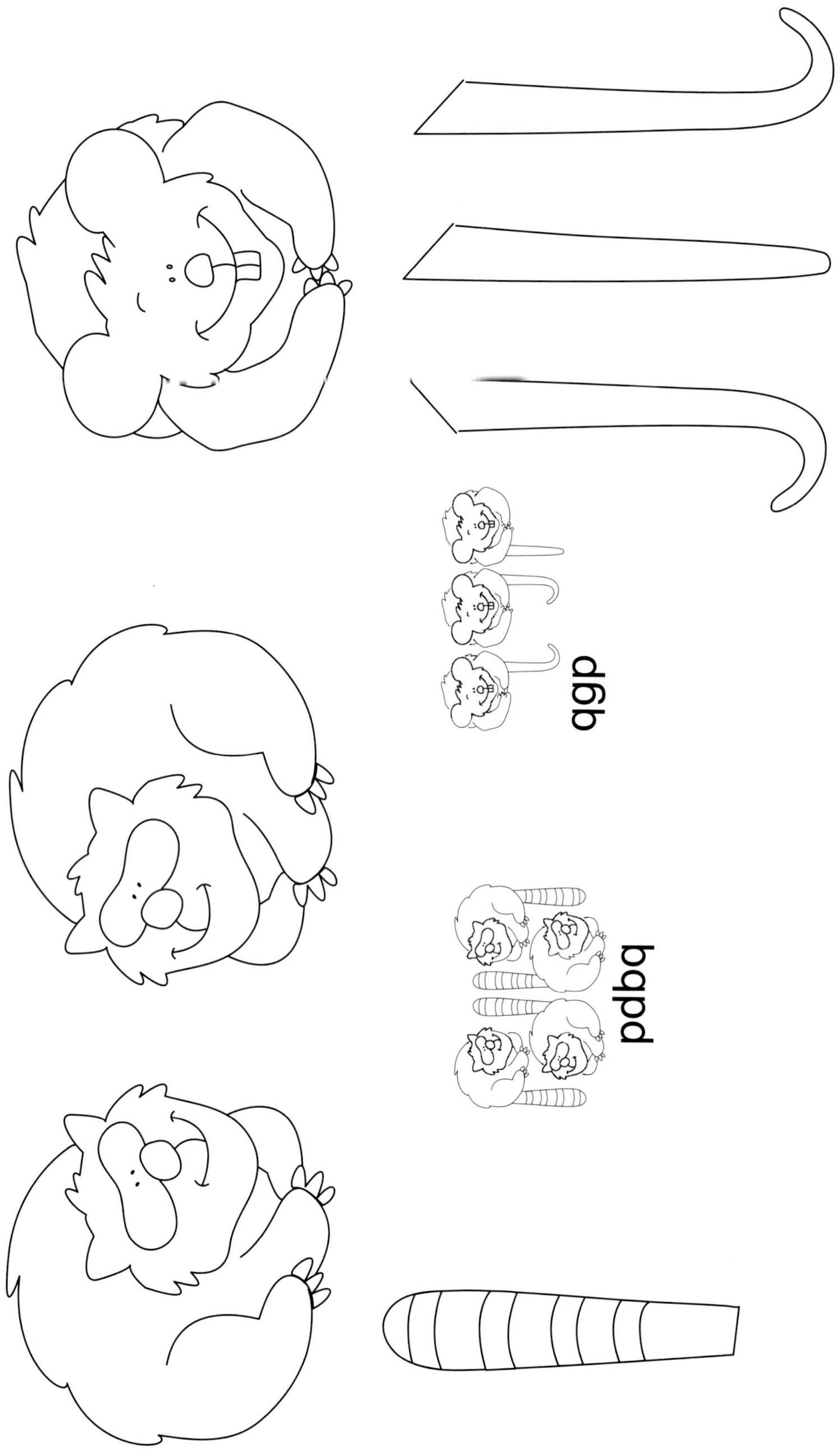
qgp
pdbq

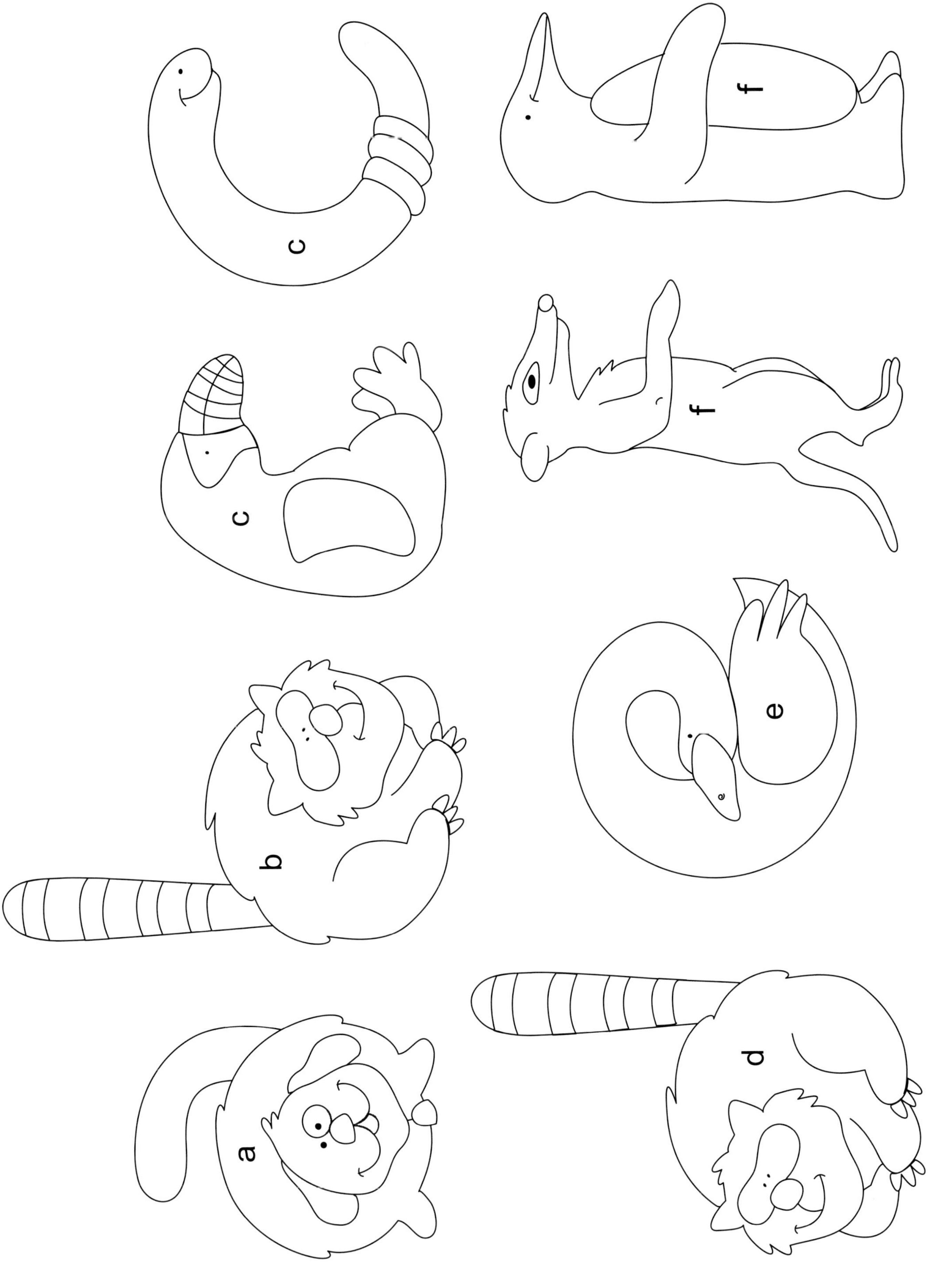
a
b
c
c
d
e
f
f

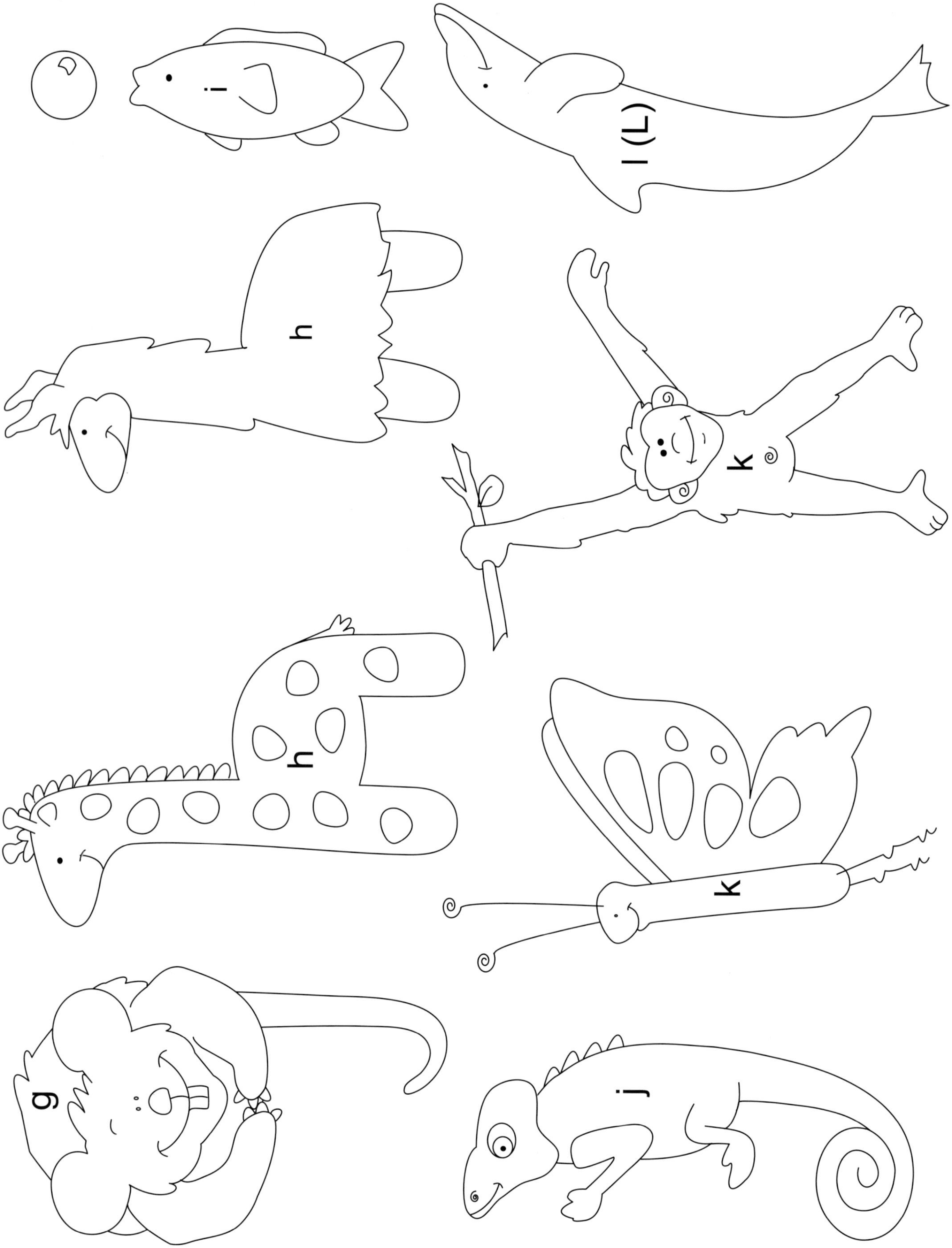
i
l (L)
h
k
h
k
g
j

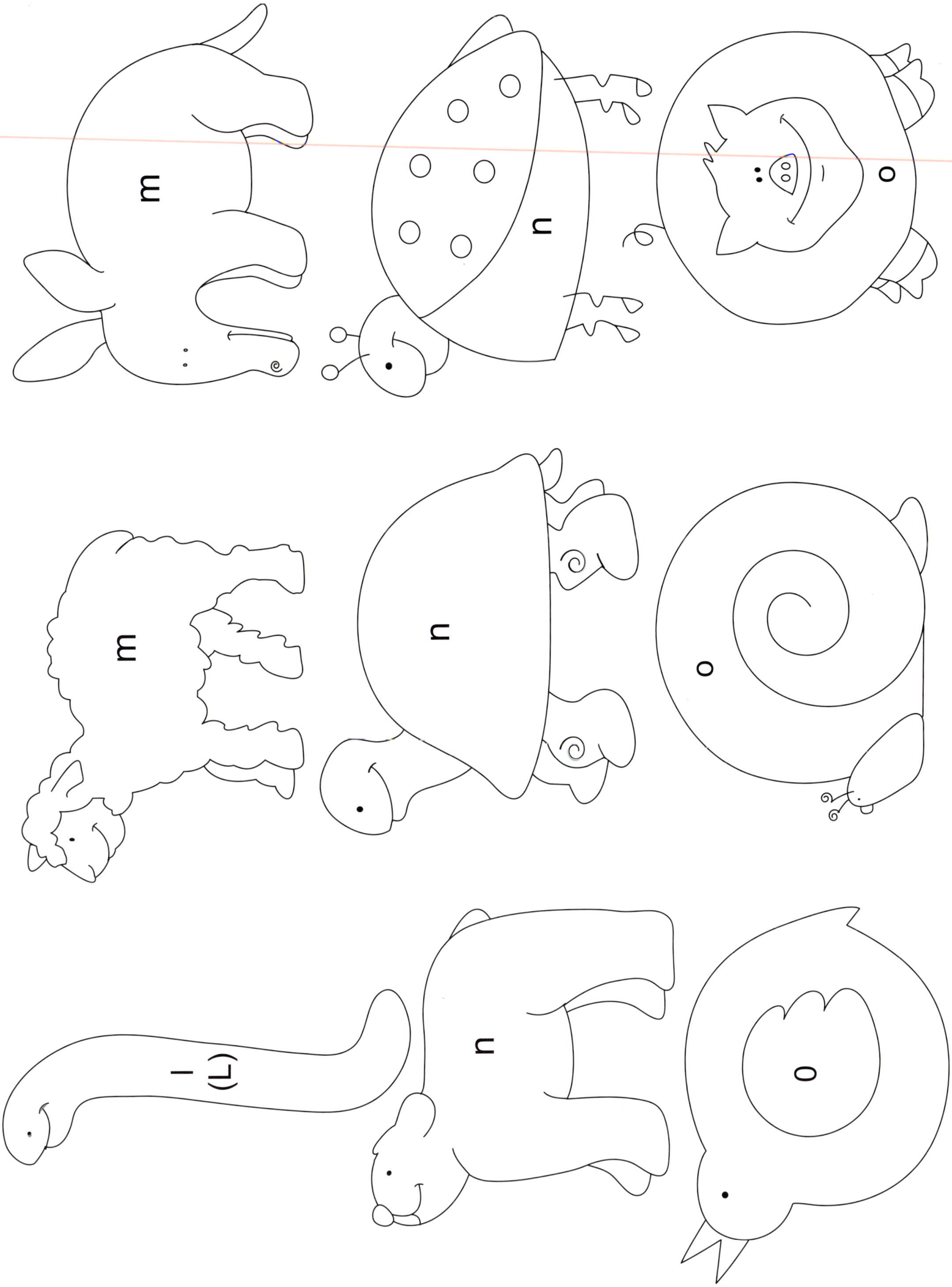
m
n
o
m
n
o
l
(L)
n
o

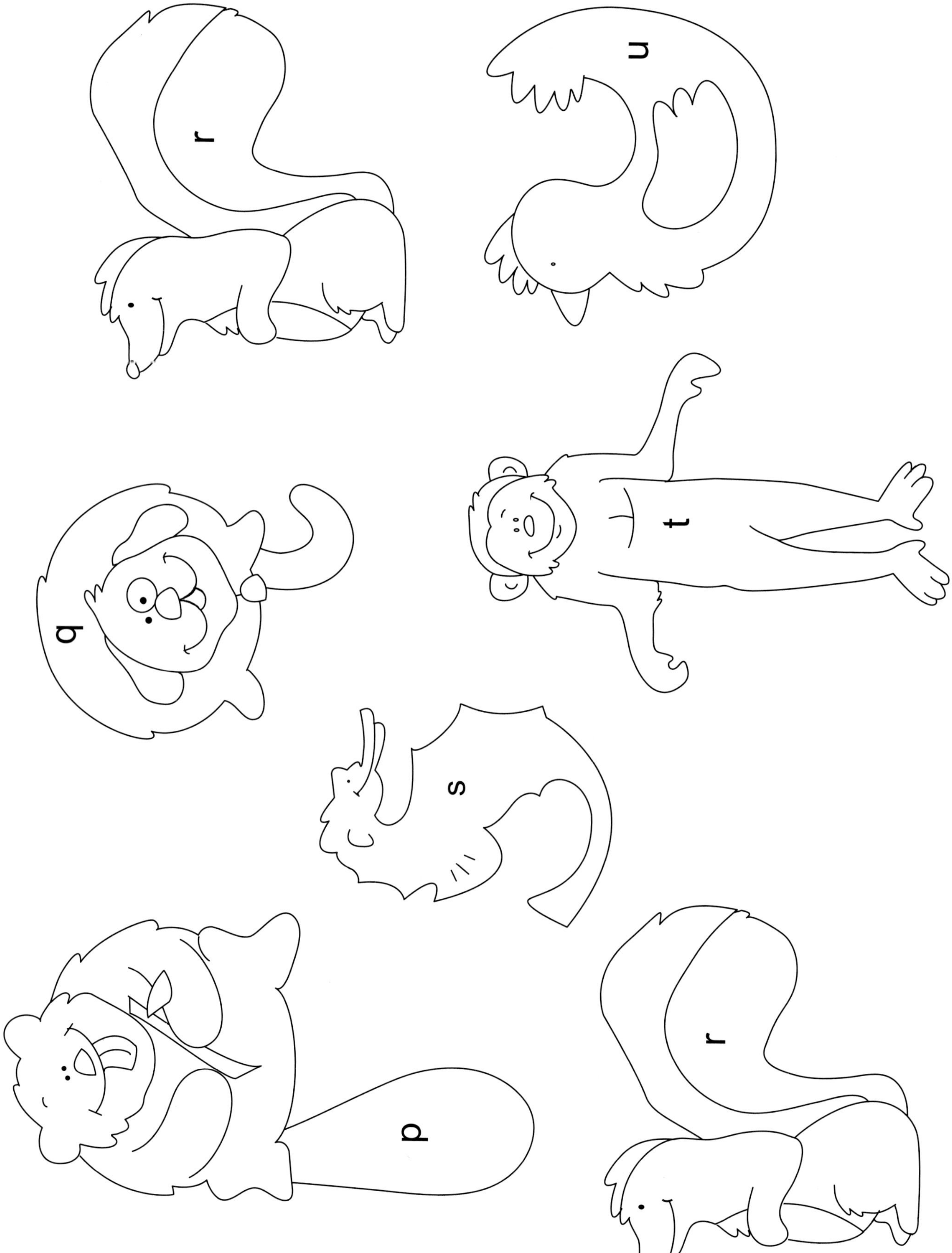
p
q
r
s
t
u
r

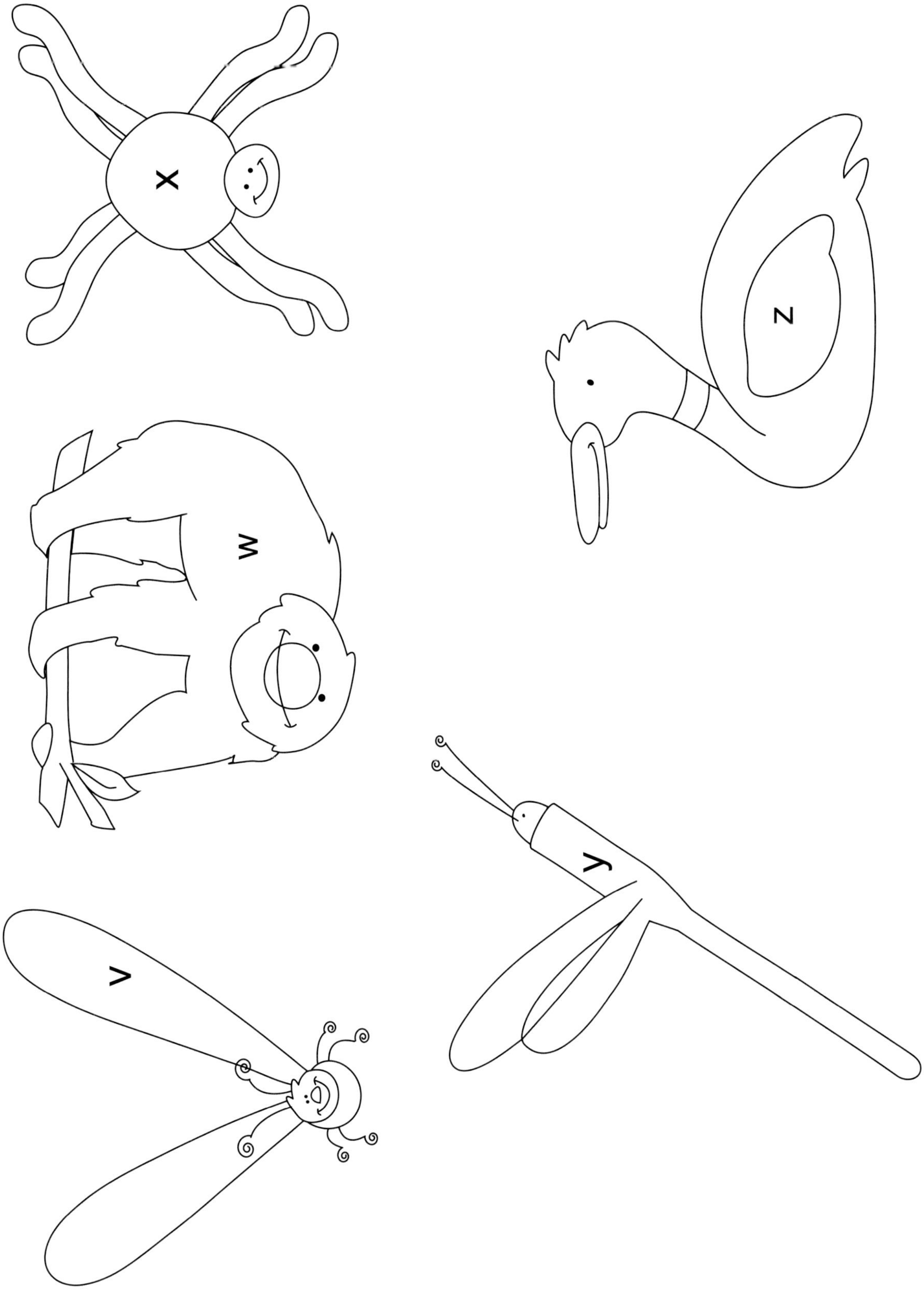
x
z
w
y
v

"Olivia" template

Place name or noun here

Place outline letters here

Place animal here

Place name or noun here

Place name or noun here

Place name or noun here

Place name or noun here

Place name or noun here

A B C D E F G H I
J K L M N O P Q
R S T U V W X Y Z
a b c d e f g h i j
k l m n o p q r s
t u v w x y z

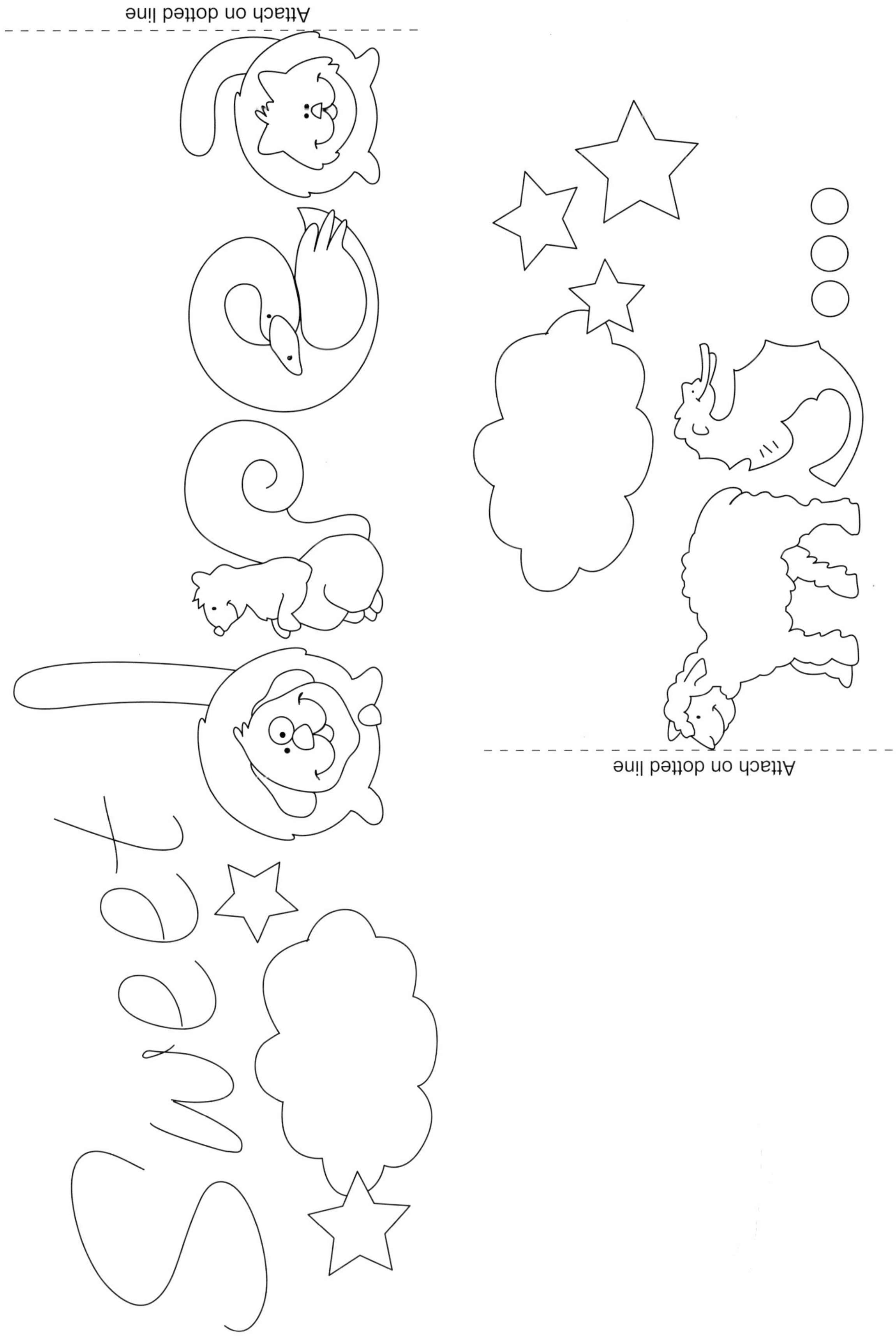
Attach on dotted line
Sweet
Attach on dotted line

Happy

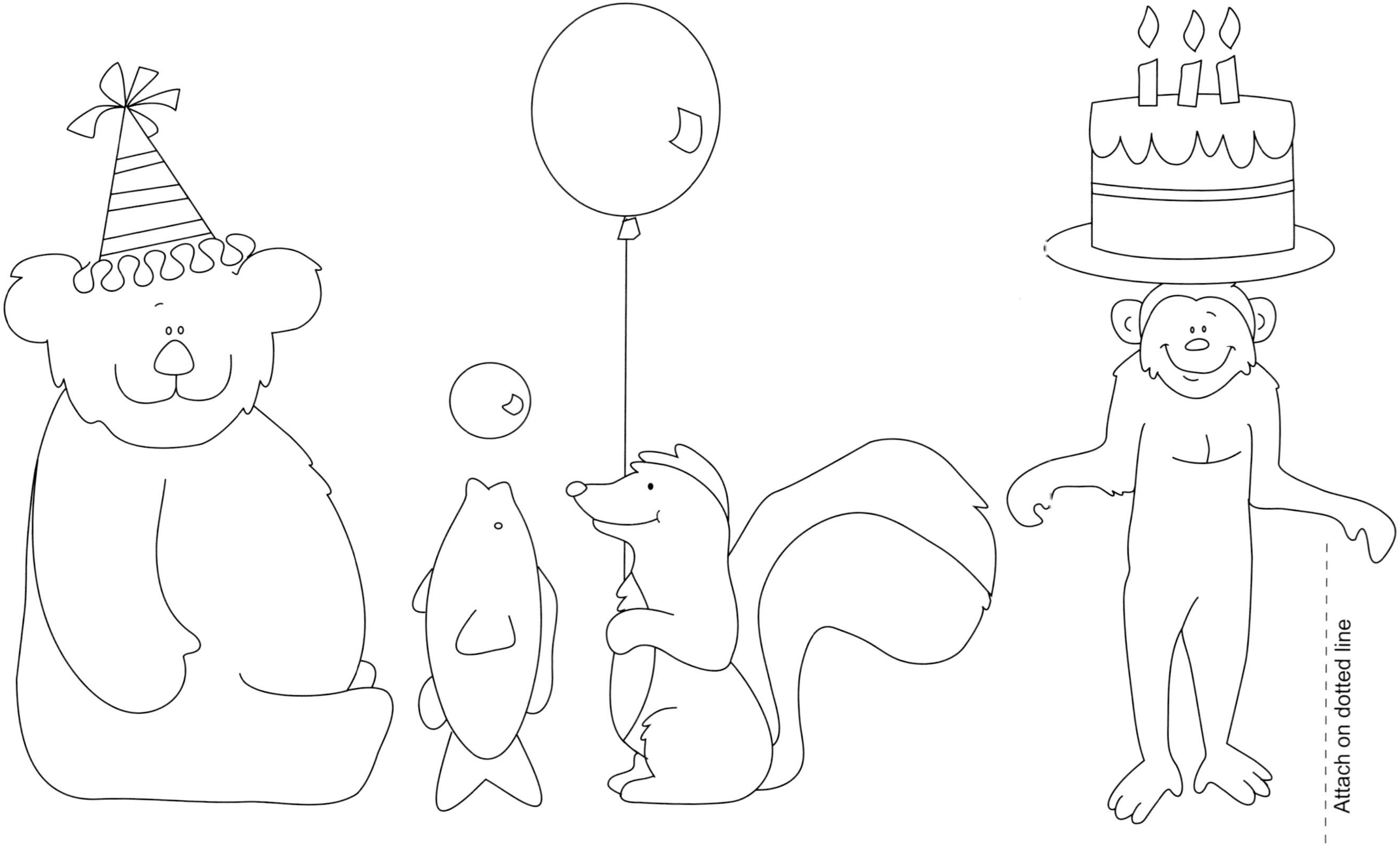

Attach on dotted line

Attach on dotted line

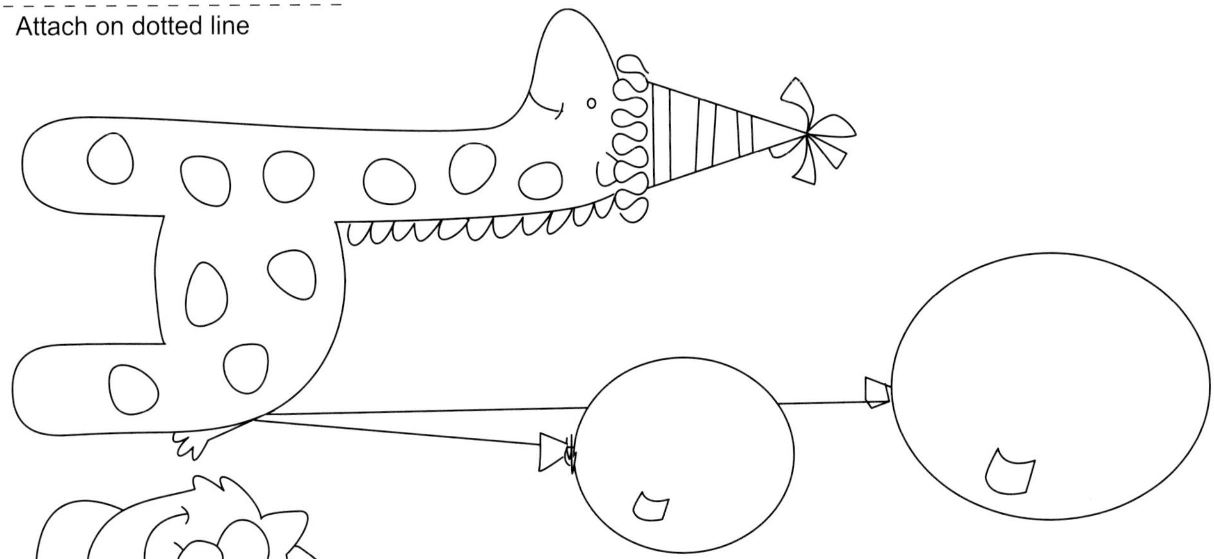

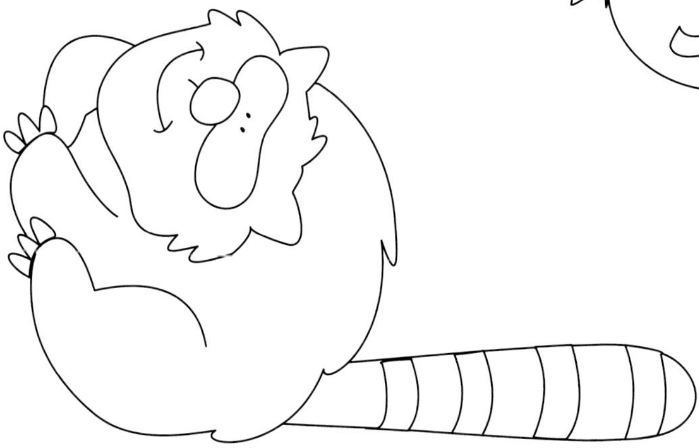

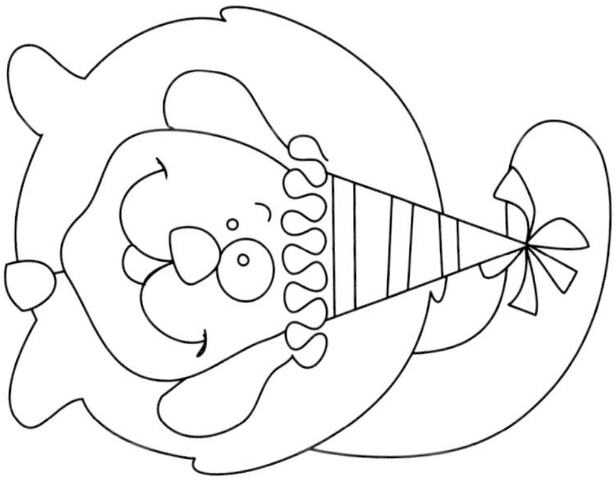

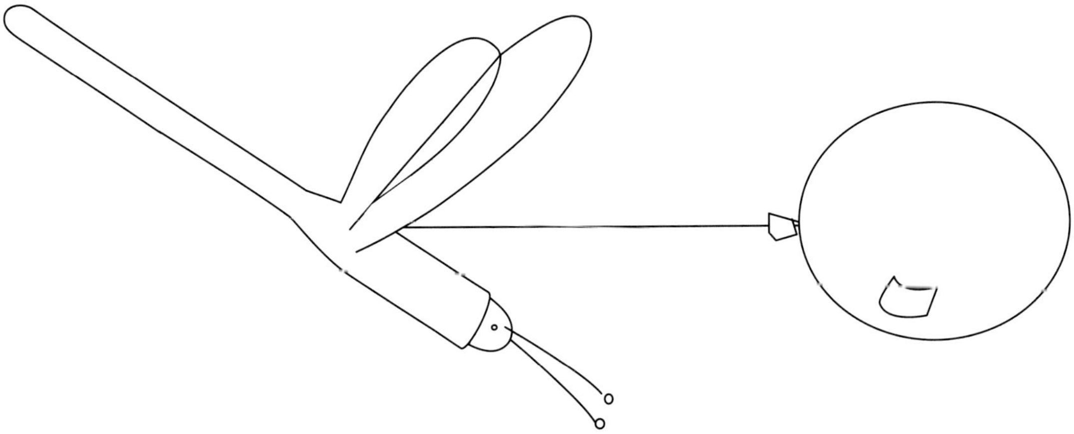

Notes

Use these pages to test the length of your names and sketch your designs.